For Nick, Annwyn, Charles
and David – with all my love

Acknowledgements

Special thanks are due to Diane Barratt and to the staff and pupils of Riddings Infant School who first gave me the opportunity to work with storytelling. Without their enthusiasm for stories and their encouragement, this book would not exist. Thanks also to John Bonham of Riddings Junior School, Ewart Gibbs and Alison Laidlaw at Leys Farm Junior School and Maria O'Hara at Enderby Road Infant School and to their hard working staff and superb children. Much of what is contained here was first tried out in their schools. Thanks also to North Lincolnshire LEA who have encouraged and facilitated an innovative approach to emotional well-being.

As always, my thanks to Nick for encouragement, belief and excellent editing skills.

Contents

Preface   9

1.   The Importance of Stories and Storytelling   11

2.   How to Tell Stories   19

3.   Traditional Tales   33

4.   Creating Unique Stories   47

5.   Children as Storytellers   57

6.   Stories and Thinking Skills   71

7.   Stories and the Environment   85

8.   Sacred Stories   95

9.   Storytelling across the Curriculum   105

10. Stories and Emotional Literacy   119

11. Storytelling and Reflection   131

Appendix 1: Sources   145
Appendix 2: Useful Addresses   147
References   149
Subject Index   151
Author Index   157

List of stories

1. Storytelling suggestion: The Story of Today   17

2. Storytelling suggestion: Little Red Riding Hood   29

3. Storytelling suggestion: The Three Feathers   44

4. Harry and the Guinea Pigs' Hutch   50

    Storytelling suggestion: Benno and the Beasts   54

5. Storytelling suggestion: The Three Little Pigs   66

6. Storytelling suggestion: Rumpelstiltskin   78

    Storytelling suggestion: Tom Tit Tot   81

7. Storytelling suggestion: Beira, Queen of Winter   92

8. The Story of Guru Nanak   98

    Never Again   101

    Storytelling suggestion: One of My Geese is Missing
    (The Story of St Werburga)   102

9. The Death of Sigurd the Powerful   107

    Storytelling suggestion: The Wolf and the Seven
    Little Kids   114

    Storytelling suggestion: Dear Child   116

10. Storytelling suggestion: Hansel and Gretel   128

11. Storytelling suggestion: The Selkie Wife   141

Preface

I was working with highly troubled teenaged girls when I first became aware of the power of stories. The girls were in local authority care. At the time I was studying for an MA in Psychoanalytic Observation and, as I read the work of the analyst Bruno Bettelheim on fairy tales, I realised that these girls had missed out on many of the great children's stories.

So I did a project on children's stories with the girls. Highly aggressive young people who would usually refuse to work or hurl books across the room – or at us – sat entranced for hours, listening to children's stories. They produced high quality academic work based on what they had heard – and they also related on a powerful emotional level to the stories I read them. The stories were therapeutic for these girls in the best and broadest sense – they were good for them.

At that point I was still reading the stories to the girls. After studying group dynamics and with a background in special needs teaching, I became attracted to the idea of putting the book down and telling the stories instead. As any storyteller will attest, if you want to learn how to tell stories, you actually have to start doing it. So I began to tell stories, to my own children, to the children I worked with and to the teachers I was training. I began to discover for myself the power, the creativity, the sheer joy of telling stories to a group of listeners.

Now I use stories and storytelling as a crucial part of my work as an education advisor and coach, encouraging creativity, effective learning and positive mental health in children and teachers. I have told stories to hundreds and hundreds of children and adults. It is rare for a group of children not to listen spellbound to simple stories, simply told. It is not a difficult skill to acquire – all teachers have the basic skills necessary to tell stories and for the most part lack only the confidence to begin. I am not a professional storyteller – just a teacher and advisor who loves stories and who believes that storytelling is one of the best tools any teacher can have.

This book is intended to help you find the confidence to start telling stories – it will also give you plenty of stories to try out and adapt for yourself. I will explore ways of using stories to enrich the curriculum and to enhance your own pleasure in teaching and learning. I will encourage you to assist the children you teach to become storytellers too and help you become aware of the social and emotional benefits of storytelling as well as the academic benefits.

I will give practical advice for starting out as a storyteller and lots of suggestions for how to build stories into the life of the classroom and the school. Try out the ideas and the stories – relax, enjoy yourself, learn as you go along and participate in an ancient human skill – telling stories.

1.

The Importance of Stories and Storytelling

Humans have always told stories. It is one of the things that makes us human and distinguishes us from other creatures. Round the campfire in the evenings, long before television was invented, people told stories to one another. Stories were used to pass on real events, history and family connections, and also to entertain. They were used to teach children and to hand down values and customs from generation to generation. Long before writing, the only culture was oral, spoken culture. To tell stories is to participate, and to help children to participate, in one of the most ancient human customs.

Storytelling has also been part of formal education for many years. In the nineteenth century, student teachers were trained to tell stories. Stories have obvious significance in the teaching of literacy, but they are also important in other curriculum areas. Stories can be an invaluable tool for developing speaking and listening skills and as a stimulus for discussion or for philosophy and thinking skills. Stories can assist the development of social awareness and help children to build up an emotional vocabulary. History and geography, science, religious education (RE) and even maths can all come alive through stories.

The beauty of storytelling in the classroom is that it works at different levels at the same time. Teachers are under pressure today to 'deliver' excellent basic skills, high academic results and emotionally literate and socially skilled children with highly developed thinking skills! Telling stories can contribute to all those areas at the same time. Listening to stories and telling stories can reduce stress in the classroom, promote literacy, speaking and listening skills, help children to develop thinking strategies and promote their social and emotional development – and all while they engage in a rewarding and enjoyable activity.

What kind of stories do we tell?

Today, the word 'story' has many different uses and this book will explore various kinds of story and storytelling. There are traditional stories, like The Three Little Pigs or Little Red Riding Hood, which form part of our children's cultural heritage. It is of course important for children to hear stories from other cultures. It is also important for children to hear stories from their own culture, and the traditional stories often called 'fairy tales' are part of the European cultural heritage. Such stories are a unique form of art, derived from the oral tradition which preceded written literature and they are a perfect first 'art form' for children to encounter and respond to.

Then there are sacred stories, told by the great storytellers like Jesus or Buddha. These are the stories that hand on values and beliefs from generation to generation and which also form part of our children's cultural and religious heritage. Whether or not we are practising members of a faith community, the stories of the Bible, the Koran and other great religious texts form part of our foundation for thinking about the world and for deciding on our own spiritual beliefs and values. Fewer adults and children today seem aware of the original significance of major religious festivals such as Easter, and this indicates a failure to pass on the central Christian story and leaves us poorer as a nation.

'Story' can also be used to mean 'anecdote' and it is this kind of storytelling that children practise first and with which adults are often most comfortable. The story of an awful trip to work through appalling traffic, the story of the last Ofsted inspection and how we survived – this kind of storytelling happens all the time in homes and staff rooms around the country and it is an important starting point for developing the skills of the storyteller.

'Story' can also be used to refer to a sequence of events during a lesson. I use a kind of storytelling that summarises all the skills and strengths children have displayed in the course of a day or a session, and whether in written or oral form, this is a useful kind of story for children to explore and experience.

Psychologists also use the word 'story' to refer to the explanations that we give ourselves about our lives and events and this kind of reflective story will also be discussed. The stories children tell themselves about themselves as learners and about their experiences in school can have profound affects on their happiness and success, not just in academic areas but more widely as they grow and develop as individuals. Paying attention to this kind of story in the classroom can help children develop a positive sense of themselves as learners and build on their successes as well as preparing them for later life – the goal of an all round education.

Storytelling is different from reading stories

Good stories are important for children, however they are delivered. My children watch the Walt Disney version of Beauty and the Beast as well as reading it in the Ladybird version and hearing me tell them my own version of it. My teenager has read adult retellings of the same fairy tale by an author called Robin McKinley and loves them, as do I.

I do not wish to suggest that we should stop *reading* stories to children. Reading aloud is always an important and valuable thing to do. However, storytelling is also valuable and important and it is much less common. Being *told* a story has elements to it that are not present when a book is read aloud.

Storytelling is enjoyable

Adults and children love hearing stories told aloud. Whether it is racial memories of sitting by the campfire or just a fundamental human need, people love hearing storytellers. There has been an upsurge of interest in professional storytelling in the past twenty years and it is now possible to hear storytellers at the Barbican and other London theatres as well as in schools and clubs up and down the country – some of these events are for children but many are now intended exclusively for adults. Hearing stories told is profoundly enjoyable.

Teachers tend to feel vaguely guilty when doing things that are 'fun'. We shouldn't. Recent studies by psychologists have shown that positive enjoyment improves learning. The psychologist Martin Seligman quotes a study of four-year-olds doing a maths test (Seligman 2003, p.36). One group was asked to think of something really happy that had happened recently and then given the test. Another group was given neutral instructions. The children asked to think of a happy event performed better at the maths test.

Building positive emotion is one of the most important tasks of those working with young children and a vital one for educators. Happy children learn better – it is as simple as that – and being told stories is something that makes children happy.

Storytelling is creative

When you read a story to children the words are fixed on the page. You may edit as you read and add your own emphasis, but essentially the words are given to you ready formed. When you tell a story, by contrast, you create the story as you go. You may know some phrases by heart, but for the most part you are thinking of the words you need as you go along, demonstrating to children that you can be creative yourself, as well as asking them to be creative.

Storytelling feels scary because you are creating something unique, something that draws on who you are and what you have experienced, something that reveals part of you in the way that every work of art reveals its creator to the world. Telling a story creates a unique work of art in front of children and demonstrates to them that this may be scary but it is something that you are prepared to do for them. You show them by example that taking creative risks is not only survivable, it is enjoyable too.

Storytelling is responsive

When you read a book to children, the author of the words almost certainly did not know your class of children. The words the children hear are those of a stranger. When you tell children a story, they hear the words of a trusted adult who knows them well and who knows what kind of day it has been and how they are feeling and who can put all of that knowledge and understanding into the story she is telling. When you tell a story, you will find you naturally alter the style and the content in response to the reactions of your listeners. Relate a tale on a quiet, studious morning and you will find you tell it in a certain way, emphasising particular words and events. Tell the same story on a hot, bad-tempered afternoon and you will tell it differently because you are responding to the moods and emotions of your listeners. This is one way of communicating to children your understanding of them and it is a very important way of helping children to feel safe and cared about.

Storytelling is active

When you tell stories, children are not passive recipients but active participants in the creative process. As a storyteller, you respond to your listeners constantly, so the children are in fact helping you to create the story. They are not watching you create so much as experiencing the creative process alongside you.

Later in the book I will explore ways of developing this aspect of storytelling and of helping children to contribute ideas and thoughts as you tell stories with them.

Storytelling is inclusive

Stories work on many levels simultaneously and children take from them what they need. Stories are, almost by definition, inclusive. I have told stories to mixed groups of adults and children where the 'children' have varied in age from three to sixteen and all present took something different, and something appropriate to them, away from the experience.

Children with particular needs may require slightly different approaches to storytelling. I told a story to a group of children with profound and multiple learning difficulties and used a multi-sensory approach, emphasising movement and sound and touch alongside the sound of the words themselves. The children's teacher said how much they obviously enjoyed the experience as they responded to the story at their own particular level. Any adaptations you make for particular children – adding props or sounds for example – will also enhance the story for all the other children present.

Storytelling is flexible

Storytelling is a skill that can be used with small groups or large groups, with adults, with children of any age or with individuals. How you tell a story will vary depending on your audience and the purpose for which you tell it, but as you develop as a storyteller you will learn to make these adaptations almost without thinking. You can tell a story to calm down a group of children or to stir them up, to comfort them or to challenge them. You can tell a story to a timid group of three-year-olds and then adapt the same story to startle and scare a group of cool Year 6 children. The only limit to storytelling is your own imagination.

Storytelling is an emotional event

Stories contain the whole range of human emotions and events – life and death, hate and love, birth and loss. When you tell a story it may be about an event that happened centuries ago, or about an imaginary event, but the story itself is happening in the here and now. The listener enters the story and experiences a little of what the characters in the story are experiencing. Through telling a range of stories you can help children to think about and recognise emotions in a safe and appropriate way.

Emotional literacy is an abstract topic that can be approached in a very concrete way through storytelling and a chapter will be devoted to thinking about how to do this.

Storytelling precedes story writing

Just as humans learned to tell stories before they learned to write novels, it is appropriate for children to have the opportunity to tell stories before they are required to write them down. Inventing characters, sequencing events, building tension and suspense are not the same skills as punctuation or spelling. The latter are important, but can get in the way of composition. Freeing children from the need to write everything down can allow them to flourish as creative artists in their own right. Teachers I work with are often surprised by the children who come into their own as storytellers – it is often not children who would shine in a traditional 'literacy' context.

When you tell stories to children without a book in your hand you underline this distinction between the oral and the written culture and

2.

How to Tell Stories

I explained in the first chapter that all stories are important whether they are read to children, watched on video or listened to on CDs or audio tapes. However, there is something quite distinct about a story that is told by a storyteller.

When you read a story to children, you read the author's words. A good reader adds expression and may edit as they read but, essentially, it is a story told by someone who does not know your class and is not there, on that day, responding to thirty faces and thirty personalities. In contrast, when you tell a story you are responding, consciously and unconsciously, to your listeners. You will pick a story that seems 'right' for that day and for that group of children. You will also tell it in a way that seems to fit the mood of the moment, or the mood that you wish to create.

There are as many different ways of telling a story as there are story-tellers. Think of how people tell jokes. A good joke is simply a funny short story. I heard someone say that the difference between jokes and stories is that all good jokes are stories but not all good stories are jokes! People tell the same joke in their own style, changing a word here, an emphasis there. Practise recalling and retelling the jokes you hear – it is a good first step in storytelling.

While it may take many years to become a professional storyteller, you do not have to be a professional to tell a good story. Before television and radio, stories were told in the evenings to pass the time and even today we tell stories to one another all the time, in the staff room, at home at the end of the day, after the holidays.

Where to start

A good place to start storytelling is with a story that is a favourite of yours or that you already know quite well. For those who teach younger children, I recommend starting off with The Three Little Pigs. It has a simple structure and lots of repetition, which makes it easier to remember. It is also a good model to use when adapting a more complex story to tell aloud as it has all the right components for a good oral story – simple language, plenty of repetition: 'I'll huff and I'll puff and I'll blow your house in', and alliteration: it is the *big bad* wolf who comes along. When I retell this story, I leave out the complicated section about going to the fair and the milk churn. I move straight from the wolf's failure to blow down the brick house to his climb up to the roof. No child has ever objected, because I retain what they feel to be the essential parts of the story.

This is an important point to remember when you are retelling a story. You can change things to suit yourself – you are the storyteller, you are in charge, you are the artist creating something new. It may be a well-known story, but that is no reason why you cannot exercise your own creativity and alter anything you like. There are many different versions of the most well-known stories and each storyteller adds his or her own variation – that is part of the oral tradition.

You can change words, characters, setting. Of course, if you change too much it becomes another story entirely, but there is no reason why you shouldn't do that too. It would be fun, with older children, to take The Three Little Pigs and say, 'I'm bored with pigs, what else shall we have today instead?'. That is precisely what the authors of *The Three Little Wolves and the Big Bad Pig* (Trivizas and Oxenbury 1993) have done and it works very well. My son told me the story of The Three Little Cars and the Big Bad Shark when he was younger.

Learning to tell a story

It is important to realise that there is a difference between recitation and storytelling. If you learn a poem, you recite it by heart, word for word, as it was written. Storytelling is not like this. You are not trying to recall a story word for word. Rather, think of the story as having fixed points or phrases which you do recall. Phrases like 'I'll huff and I'll puff' or 'not by the hair on my chinny chin chin'. You learn these and use them at the right points. They are like scaffolding for the rest of the story. You might also want to decide on an opening line and a last line that always remain the same – or not if you prefer. In between, however, you make up the words that you need as you go along.

This means that you can tailor the story and adapt it, adding details here and there to suit you and the children. One day, the first pig might meet a man called John carrying a bundle of straw and you catch the eye of the John in your class. Or you might decide to balance out the gender of the characters and the second pig can meet a woman carrying a bundle of sticks. Children enjoy this kind of playful adaptation, and it models for them a lightness and a willingness to be creative. It also means that the children know that this retelling is unique, that you have created something that is just for them.

Read through any story you wish to tell a few times and then put the book or written version away. Practise retelling it by yourself a few times, refreshing your memory if you need to. Then tell it to your audience. Don't worry if you forget things – if it is a well-known story the children will probably remind you. If it is less well known, they won't notice anyway.

Creating the silence

Though it may at first seem paradoxical, there is an important link between stories and silence. Though stories are about words and speech and sound, they cannot take place against a backdrop of noise. For a story to be told, there must first be silence. Stories start with silence, contain important moments of complete stillness and end in silence. Silence, moreover, is not something that just happens. It is not primarily an absence of noise. In the context of storytelling especially, silence is something that we must *create*.

The ability to be totally still is an important part of storytelling. Words need silence around them or they are meaningless. It is in the pauses in a story that enjoyment and anticipation build up and the story itself sinks into our hearts and minds and makes connections with what we have already experienced and learned.

A storyteller will talk about 'letting the story form inside you' before you tell it. This pause before you start a story is crucial. You take a breath and tune in to your listeners, to the environment, to the mood of the group around you and to your own emotional state – and then you begin.

There are simple techniques you can use that can help you and the children (or any other audience for that matter) become still and quiet as you prepare for a story to start. One is to light a candle. Get it out, very slowly and deliberately. Carry it to a prominent position in the room. Say nothing and every eye will be on you at once and the silence will start as they watch, fascinated, while you light it. Or sit them down and then stand, slowly and walk to a cupboard. Open it deliberately, carefully and take out a beautiful scarf. Carry the scarf back to you chair and look at it for a moment. Pause and then put it on with a flourish. Sit up, look at them … and begin. Your slow, deliberate movements, *your* silence and stillness, will create a silence and stillness in the room. You model how to be quiet, how to be comfortable with stillness.

Another technique I have used effectively from reception to Year 6 is a rain stick. I have one made of transparent plastic (from a well-known early years shop). The children watch, absorbed and quiet, as I turn the stick and the wheels spin as the brightly coloured beads rush past them. When the beads have all fallen, I pause for a second, then another, letting the silence build up before turning the stick over once more. When the silence is complete, I put down the rain stick and begin the story.

When you are telling a story, too, don't be afraid to let silences build up – hold the children's gaze with your own or fix your attention on a single prop and you will find that they gaze at it intensely as well. A long pause before a sudden noise can have children jumping in pleasurable terror as you startle them with a sudden loud 'squeeeeak' or 'splaaaaaaaash'. The anticipation, the silent pause, adds to the pleasure.

Using props

Using very simple props to retell a story is also a good way to start. The props can be very simple indeed and nothing like what they represent. Bricks, shells, sticks, can all represent the characters in a story. You could hold up three bricks and introduce them. 'Here are the three little pigs' and then put them down in front of you as you begin to tell the story. Children are happy to accept the leap of imagination necessary to see the bricks as pigs – later you can use this to introduce them to the idea of symbols, that the bricks aren't really pigs of course, they just represent pigs. Moving the bricks around on the floor will prompt you to remember the words and help you keep track of where you are in the story.

Another way to use props is to have a single object or piece of cloth that is suggestive of the story. You use this prop to introduce the story and hold and look at it while you are speaking. You might use a shell as the prop for a sea legend, for example, or a piece of red cloth for Little Red Riding Hood.

You can use the children as props, too. Stand up and walk around telling the story, while the children 'become' the straw house, or the wooden house. They can work on this in groups beforehand, thinking about how their 'straw' house will be different from their 'wooden' house. Or they can work individually, again with some prior thinking time to decide what their house will look like. Alternatively, you can challenge them to become any object in the story when you point at them and not tell them in advance which object they will have to be!

These techniques have the advantage that the children have to listen hard and watch you all the time for their cues. Working together to think of what their straw house will look like will also extend speaking and listening skills as well as creativity and thinking skills.

A story box

I use a simple story box technique that has been influenced by the Montessori based approach to religious education (RE) called Godly Play. Godly Play uses wooden figures to tell Bible stories, and the storyteller moves the figures in silence and then speaks in between that movement. The figures and the cloths are specific to each story.

When I use a story box, I use a single set of neutral props that can tell any story, sacred or traditional. A simple wooden shape can be a little pig, a princess, a hero or a saint. The simplicity of the figures and the other props means that the children's imaginations are stimulated to the full. They can 'see' their own hero, their own 'pig' when you tell the story.

I have different coloured felt cloths that 'become' the world of the story. I use a green one for traditional European stories, a yellow one for stories from Africa or Australia, a blue one for sea stories. The box also contains a candle to light, a scarf to put on and simple props like shells,

This is an example of a story box that may be used to tell any story.

wooden blocks and glass beads that can become any character. There are not too many, otherwise the box would become cluttered.

I do not always use props for each character. Often I leave out the 'wolf' or the 'monster' so that the children can put it in for themselves. I open my box very slowly, seated on the floor in a circle for preference, I put on my scarf, spread my cloth and smooth it out, light the candle and take out the first prop. And then I start.

As in Godly Play, I move the figures in silence and speak in between. This allows pools of silence to enter the story, almost without the children noticing.

When the story is finished, I follow it with a minute's silence, for thinking time. I have a small timer which I set for a minute and show to the children. They can see the seconds tick away and know that the silence has an observable end, which again reduces anxiety. An egg timer would also work well. I have never known children struggle to maintain complete silence for that minute.

This quiet approach to storytelling works well before a thinking or 'philosophy' session because it helps the children to relax and feel calm. It is therefore going to help them with lateral thinking and openness and the ability to listen to other opinions.

Drama

There is an important difference between acting and storytelling. When you tell a story, you may choose to do the voices of the different characters, to add colour and life to the retelling. But you may not. A quieter telling, that speaks the characters' words in a simple, quite neutral way, can also be effective.

I have heard storytellers who regard it as important not to use gesture or dramatic voices in their stories. Alternatively, I have heard others who move between telling the story, as the narrator, and who then 'become' a character in their story, acting out a particular scene. These are much more dramatic retellings.

There is no right or wrong here. What you do and how you do it will gradually emerge out of your interests, skills and personality. People talk of 'finding your own voice' and this is the case whether you are writing stories or telling stories. You may wish to use gesture or to sit very still and let the words speak. If you are musical, you may wish to incorporate music into your stories. Borrowing tunes and fitting new words to them is a simple thing to do and I have a few stories that employ simple songs in this way.

If you are artistic, you may wish to make masks or a painting to look at while you tell the story. Follow your own strengths and your stories will come to life.

Repetition

The other important aspect of learning to tell a story is repetition – telling the same story again and again, either to different groups of children (or adults) or the same group on different occasions. The story will change each time but more and more it will become part of you, something that you 'know' in quite a profound way.

In this country, we have come to have a sense that children need constant novelty, that they will become bored by repetition. Most certainly this is not true of younger children, who have a great need for rhythm and predictability. I am not sure that it is always the case even for older children. Repetition, if what is repeated is worth listening to in the first place, can be deeply satisfying for all people, regardless of age. Think of how good it feels to repeat the same rituals at Christmas time, or to reread a favourite novel or watch a much loved film. Children do not seem to mind watching the same video again and again or playing the same computer game – why should they not hear the same story told to them? Repetition, provided it is balanced with change and variety, provides security and can help alleviate anxiety.

Children with special needs, children going through stressful experiences, or just children feeling rather daunted by the demands of growing up, can all benefit immensely from the thoughtful repetition of favourite stories. However, healthy, happy children usually enjoy repetition just as much.

In the Waldorf education system in Norway, the school day ends for children up to the age of seven with storytelling around the fire by candlelight. The same traditional story is told every day for a week. This allows the children to get to know the story really well, to think about it and the issues it raises for them. It also allows the storyteller to get to know the story thoroughly so that it enters her repertoire and can be recalled and retold at any time.

Try this with your class. Tell them that this week you are going to have the same story – explain that it is an experiment. What does it feel like having the same story every day and knowing that tomorrow you will end the day in the same way as today? Invite their thoughts and responses. Perhaps your class has a high need for variety and will not relish that degree of repetition. Or perhaps they will enjoy the predictability, and the challenge, of spotting what small changes you make each time that you tell it.

Hearing a story so often will also, of course, provide them with a very good foundation for starting to tell the story themselves. You can tell the story in different ways each time you tell it, if you choose. One day you could use props, another day you could change a detail about a character, or have the children say one of the lines for you. You will think of other ways of making small changes whilst keeping the essential nature of the story the same.

Involving the audience

Some stories, such as The Three Little Pigs or The Three Billy Goats Gruff, simply cry out for audience participation. You do not have to prompt children to join in with the well-known phrases. You can also involve them in other ways. When I retell Little Red Riding Hood, I first ask the children to suggest what Mother packs into the basket for Grandma. I limit this to three or four items and when I tell the story I include the children's ideas, repeating, at frequent intervals, the phrase 'with her basket of [e.g. eggs, cake and spaghetti]'. Children love to have their suggestions used and there is natural humour in the weird combinations that they give you that you and they can enjoy together. They also like to test your memory.

Another way I use to draw children into a story, and to hone their listening skills, is to give them something to listen out for. Telling Little Red Riding Hood, for example, I might ask the children to invent a tree shape and to remember it. Then, whenever I use the phrase 'deep dark wood' they have to get into the shape of the tree they first thought of. That would be fun and fairly chaotic. Getting children to join in with well-known phrases or animal noises is also fun but can be noisy.

If you are wanting to calm and quieten the children, such techniques are best saved for another time. A quieter way to encourage listening and involvement is to give the children a gesture to make each time you say a certain word or phrase. Wherever possible I use gestures from British Sign Language. Even if there are no signing children in your school, this is one way of beginning to build children's awareness of another kind of language and to build a vocabulary in sign language for when they do meet a deaf child or an adult whose first language is sign language. My other reason for using signs from British Sign Language is that I think they are beautiful and provide a wonderful visual component to stories.

In the story of Little Red Riding Hood, the little girl forgets her mother's warnings. I repeat the word 'forgot' numerous times in my version and might teach children the sign to go with it, a closed hand pointing to the head, moved away with fingers opening, as if you are literally taking something out of your head. (Details of a good first dictionary of signs, *Start to Sign!*, can be found in Appendix 2 and References, Magill and Hodgson (2000).) The children have to listen very carefully for the word and each time they hear it they join in making the sign for 'forgot'. This both helps to hold their attention and draws them into the story in a calm and thoughtful way.

The school as a community of storytellers

One excellent way of learning to tell a story is to have the opportunity to tell it numerous times in quick succession. If a member of staff learnt one story and then went around the school telling it to each group of children they would find they had learned that story so thoroughly that they could probably tell it again, without practice, even months later. It would be inside them, *their* story. If each member of staff had the opportunity to do this, the school would then have quite a repertoire of oral stories that the children could listen to and enjoy, time and again. If 'member of staff' were extended to include enthusiastic learning support assistants, care-takers, office and kitchen staff, think how widely the community of storytellers would spread.

An added benefit of such an approach would be that relationships would be developed and enhanced across the school. Telling a story to a group of children is quite an intimate event. You get to know them and they get to know you in a very warm and positive way. Teachers and other staff would get to know children they had not taught directly and, in this way, the community spirit of the school would grow and develop. If support and other staff were involved too, the children would see a differ-ent side to dinner ladies and office staff and again, positive relationships would be developed between adults and children.

This practice would also help children at the transition point between teachers. They would already know their new teacher as a storyteller and, for anxious children especially, this might make a real difference to how they settle into a new class.

A school might set aside one day every term or every year as storytell-ing day and the children could hear and the adults tell as many stories as possible in that day. Different storytellers could carry a prop or wear a distinctive item of clothing – a hat, a shawl, a bright jumper – and go from class to class telling their story.

It would not be a big step then to encourage the children to start developing as storytellers too. In structured ways, as will be explained in a later chapter, the children can start developing their own oral storytelling skills, which will boost their confidence, enhance their speaking and listening skills and provide an excellent foundation for their written work.

There is in fact a time of year when it would be perfect to hold this kind of 'storytelling day'. The Society for Storytelling (details in Appendix 2) promotes National Storytelling Week. It has been running for about ten years now and is held during the first week in February every year. It is the perfect way to brighten up a gloomy time of year. The aim is for as much live oral storytelling, professional or amateur, to take place at one time and to raise awareness of our oral storytelling tradition.

One school I work with holds their own story festival to coincide with National Storytelling Week. They invite in a professional storyteller but, crucially, both the teachers and the children also tell stories in the course of the week. Stories are told both in assembly and in classrooms, the children work with stories, play with stories and think about stories. Videos are made of the events to share with the school's companion school in China. It is a highlight of the school year.

Storytelling suggestion

Try telling this version of Little Red Riding Hood in different ways on successive days. For example, you might use a red cloth on one day, simple props or a story box on another day, encourage lots of audience participation on the third day, change a character on the fourth day and on the fifth day, ask the children to become the deep dark wood and to make the shape of a tree each time you repeat that phrase.

Little Red Riding Hood

Once upon a time, a little girl lived with her mother on the edge of a deep dark forest. She was called Little Red Riding Hood. She was kind and everybody loved her.

One day her mother asked her to visit her grandmother who lived on the other side of the deep dark forest, and who had not been well. Little Red Riding Hood's mother packed a basket with delicious things for Grandmother to eat – freshly baked bread and chocolate cakes, biscuits and fruit pies [ask the children for their own suggestions here] – and she gave it to Little Red Riding Hood.

'Now remember,' said Little Red Riding Hood's mother, 'don't stray from the path, don't dawdle on the way and DON'T talk to strangers!'

Little Red Riding Hood promised not to forget and, picking up her basket of freshly baked bread and chocolate cakes, biscuits and fruit pies, she walked happily along the path into the deep dark forest.

She had not gone very far when who should she meet but the big bad wolf! He bowed to her, very politely, and said, 'Good morning little girl. And where would you be going?'

Little Red Riding Hood forgot that she was not to talk to strangers and said, 'I am going to visit my grandmother, sir, who lives in the white cottage on the other side of the deep dark forest. She has not been well and I am taking her this basket of freshly baked bread and chocolate cakes, biscuits and fruit pies to help her feel better.'

The big bad wolf bowed again, very politely, and suggested she might like to gather some flowers for her grandmother, too. Then he walked quickly on.

Little Red Riding Hood forgot that she was not to dawdle on her way and began to gather some flowers as the wolf had suggested. Then Little Red Riding Hood forgot that she was not to stray from the path and she wandered further and further into the deep dark forest, picking flowers as she went.

Meanwhile, the big bad wolf ran straight to Grandmother's house and knocked on the door. 'It's only me, Grandma,' he said, very politely and very sweetly, pretending to be Little Red Riding Hood.

'Lift up the latch and come in my dear,' said Grandmother.

The wolf lifted the latch, opened the door and went into the dim, dark cottage and swallowed Grandmother whole! Then he put on her spare night gown and night cap, drew the curtains and climbed into bed to wait.

It was growing late when Little Red Riding Hood finally arrived. She knocked on the door. 'It's only me, Grandma,' she called.

'Lift up the latch and come in my dear,' called the wolf, pretending to be Grandmother.

Little Red Riding Hood lifted the latch, opened the door and went into the dim, dark cottage. She looked at the shape in the bed.

'Oh Grandma,' said Little Red Riding Hood, 'what big ears you have!'

'All the better to hear you with, my dear,' replied the wolf.

'Oh Grandma,' said Little Red Riding Hood, 'what big eyes you have!'

'All the better to see you with, my dear,' replied the wolf.

'Oh Grandma,' said Little Red Riding Hood, 'what big teeth you have!'

'All the better to EAT you with my dear!' cried the wolf, and he sprang out of the bed.

Little Red Riding Hood screamed, hit the wolf with her basket, opened the door and rushed into the wood yelling at the top of her voice.

A man chopping wood heard her, ran to the cottage and chopped off the wolf's head. And out sprang Grandmother! She was alive and well but very cross at being cooped up in the wolf's tummy.

Grandmother, Little Red Riding Hood and the woodcutter went back to the cottage and ate fresh bread and chocolate cakes, biscuits and fruit pies for their supper.

Little Red Riding Hood, of course, lived happily ever after and met no more big bad wolves on the way to Grandma's house.

3.

Traditional Tales

Traditional tales hold a special place in our cultural history and in the education of children. Sometimes referred to as 'fairy tales', though they rarely contain fairies, they do have fantastic elements that enrich our everyday lives – magic and enchantment, strange beings and stranger events. They are also about the common human issues that we all experience and which children must learn to think about and live through – love and hate, death and dying, fear and separation. Traditional tales contain evil and violence but good always triumphs in the end and most traditional tales, with some exceptions, are moral tales as well as entertaining ones. Children already know that violence and evil exist. Traditional tales introduce these concepts in a safe way, in the context of a hopeful ending. They contain good characters as well as bad ones and helpful figures that allow the hero or heroine to triumph over adversity.

Traditional tales convey moral messages but indirectly. No one, and that includes children, likes to feel preached at. Traditional tales invite a child to identify with the good character rather than, as in a fable, telling the child to be good. Children can accept or decline such invitations – it is left up to them. No demands are made on the listener and they are never made to feel bad or inferior. On the contrary, it is often the smallest and the youngest character in a tale who solves the problem or saves the day and children can feel greatly encouraged by this.

The exceptions to the moral traditional tale are stories such as Jack and the Beanstalk – in the original, Jack was stealing the giant's treasure, not stealing back his father's treasure. Puss in Boots is, likewise, a tale of deception. They are still useful tales however, if only because they will stimulate children to consider ethical issues – is lying ever right? Was it all right to steal from the giant just because he was a giant? As openings for discussion, such stories cannot be improved upon.

Traditional tales are also great works of art, products of our ancient, oral culture and they are an art form that is uniquely suited to children and the school setting. They enrich children's outer and inner lives in a unique way and are a good foundation for an appreciation of more complex art and literature. Traditional tales have been written about and valued by artists such as the poet Louis MacNeice and the writers G.K. Chesterton, C.S. Lewis and J.R.R. Tolkien. They have been honed and refined over many years and are the vehicle by which cultural values have been handed down the generations. It is important for children in this country to hear the European traditional tales as well as folk tales from other cultures because they are an important part of the cultural heritage of the Western world.

Traditional tales differ from myths, to which they are related, in that they are mostly told about ordinary people. Myths are extra-ordinary – great heroes doing majestic tasks, often consorting with gods and god-desses. Traditional tales are about farmers' sons, woodcutters and little girls. The names given to the characters in traditional tales are really generic, almost nicknames: Jack, Hansel, Gretel, Little Red Riding Hood. This means that children can identify very strongly with the central char-acter in their struggles and attempts to overcome evil. The message of the traditional tale is simple but powerful – life is not easy, but you can survive and there will be good characters available to help you along the way.

The emotional power of traditional stories

Western countries are undergoing what has been described as an 'epi-demic of depression' (Seligman 1995, p.37). Not only is depression on the increase, but it is affecting people at an earlier and earlier age. Fifty years ago the average age of a first depressive illness was around thirty years. Now it is around fourteen years.

There are various theories about what is causing this epidemic but, whatever the reasons, it is clear that more and more children are being affected by mental illness. One of the factors that protects against depression is hope and that is where traditional tales can be useful. Bruno Bettelheim, a child psychologist working and writing in the later part of the twentieth century, said that traditional tales, which he called fairy tales, make a 'great and positive psychological contribution to the child's inner growth' (Bettelheim 1976, p.12). He went on to say that a true fairy tale was a tale of hope. It presented the listener with the struggles of the hero or heroine, which were metaphors for the ordinary struggles of life, and showed that these struggles could be overcome and survived. They are overwhelmingly positive tales that say to the child, or indeed the adult, you can survive this too. Bettelheim did not regard sad stories, such as The Little Match Girl or The Ugly Duckling, as true fairy tales. Fairy tales have happy endings and that is one reason why they are important for children.

A true fairy tale, according to Bettelheim, is always hopeful. It presents children with a story in which the hero or heroine finds the resources to overcome their struggles and to triumph over adversity. It is a powerful message and one that children cannot hear too often.

In some cultures, stories are seen as therapeutic. In traditional Hindu medicine a patient was given a folk story to meditate upon. The story would be one which was seen as encapsulating the patient's difficulty in some way and which would allow the patient to visualise both his problem and the means by which it might be overcome. The patient would then, like the hero of the story, overcome their difficulty.

Stories and storytelling are also, increasingly, used by therapists in our own culture but teachers do not need to be therapists to offer good things to the children they teach. Traditional tales are the product of centuries, perhaps more, of accumulated human interest and wisdom. The traditional tales that have been handed down over countless generations have lasted because they are profoundly satisfying tales, for adults as well as for children, and because they work at many levels. Stories are therapeutic because they allow the listener to find their own solutions to the problems that they face.

Traditional tales and metaphor

Stories are perfect for when children feel troubled because they work through metaphor rather than addressing issues directly. The potential

drawback of stories with an obvious 'point', like a tale about the divorce
of parents, is that they may be of limited interest to a child who is not
going through that experience and may even create anxiety that such an
event may take place where it did not exist before.

On the other hand, for a child whose parents are about to divorce or
who have divorced, the story may be too direct, too close for comfort to
be of much use. However, a group of children can listen to a story like
Hansel and Gretel and apply it to their many and varied situations. One
child, whose parents argue, may derive comfort from the fact that Hansel
and Gretel manage to survive without adult help. A child of divorced
parents may relate to how abandoned the children feel by the adults in
their lives. Another, very gentle, child may focus on the witch's cruelty
and greed and find those unfamiliar emotions rather exciting in the safe
context of the story. Children can thus interpret the metaphors of traditional tales to suit their own particular needs and the same child may
hear the same story on another day and find a completely different
meaning in it for them.

Very young children often enjoy the story of The Three Little Pigs.
This can be interpreted in many ways, but one possible meaning is the
need for children to leave behind the ability to play all day – the first two
pigs – and assume the greater responsibilities of school-aged children.
They, like the third pig, must now work hard for much of the time. It is
perhaps no coincidence that this story seems to have particular resonance
for children just starting school. It conveys both the excitement of going
into the big wide world and the dangers, i.e. the wolf. The deaths of the
first two pigs convey the truth that change is sad as well as exciting and
that old ways of life must die for new ones to take over. In this respect, a
change is like a little death and that is depicted, metaphorically, through
the deaths in the story.

It is of course possible to interpret The Three Little Pigs in other ways
and that is precisely the power of a story. It can mean different things to
each person who hears it and each person can take whatever lessons they
wish from it – or no lessons at all.

It is also quite possible for a story to affect us without us being consciously aware of it. We may simply enjoy the story without knowing
how it is working at a deeper level. If we return to a story again and again,
if we find it particularly satisfying, this is probably a clue to its importance

for us in some way. This is true of adults and also of children. Children may return to the same story repeatedly for a period and then discard it for months or years. It has served its purpose and then they move on to something else. They may return to it years later and find in it quite different meanings from when they were younger.

Traditional tales as containers for anxiety

Children's emotions can be very powerful. One of the most frightening thoughts as a child is that you are the only person to feel like this – the only person to hate a sibling, or to fear abandonment, or to feel rivalry with or resentment of a parent. Stories help children to know that they are not alone with such feelings. They present children with the range of human experience and feelings and, crucially, they have happy endings. They tell children, indirectly and powerfully, that the strong feelings they have can be survived and thought about.

Children are at a disadvantage in a society designed by and for adults. They are relatively helpless and dependent on the good will of adults for their well-being. That is fine if the adults they know are dependable but sometimes they are not. Even if the adults in a child's life are dependable now, what if something changed or the adults died? How does a child cope with the fact that sometimes its much loved parents are bad tempered and unreasonable? For children these are real anxieties and difficulties that traditional tales help them to think about and manage.

Traditional tales contain simple, one-dimensional characters. A character is either good or evil, not a confusing mixture of the two. This is part of what makes these tales comforting – they are simpler than reality. However, as a map is a simpler version of the real landscape but a useful tool for finding our way, so a traditional tale is a simple version of life but is still a useful tool for helping us to think about how we wish to live and how we might persist in the face of difficulties.

Traditional tales are peopled by giants and kings and queens that are thinly disguised metaphors for adults in general and parents in particular. Children may feel mostly positive feelings for their parents but sometimes they feel negative ones too. These feelings can worry children – they know they 'ought' to love their mother, but sometimes their mother is bad tempered or unreasonable. What do they do with these worrying, hateful feelings for the people they love and depend on, feelings which they would rather not have? Such emotions, suppressed, can lead to difficulties. Traditional tales provide an excellent and healthy container for the powerful, uncomfortable emotions that all children, and adults, feel from time to time.

The child can hate and fear the wicked stepmother in Cinderella or the horrid stepmother in Hansel and Gretel and find relief from their anxieties about hating their real mother or father. Interestingly, in early versions of Hansel and Gretel it was the children's natural mother who urged the father to abandon them. A recent radio programme suggested that abandoning infants was fairly common among poor families in the eighteenth century and earlier and that the story may therefore contain a memory of a very real anxiety felt by children through the ages.

The splitting of characters into good and bad allows the child to make sense of the fact that sometimes the adults in its life are pleasant and sometimes they are not. They can identify the 'good' mother with a fairy godmother and the 'bad' mother with the witch or evil stepmother. They can also be helped to make sense of their own confused and mixed emotions by projecting them into the tale. Those parts of the child with which they are not comfortable – hate, aggression, envy or the capacity for cruelty – can be projected onto the bad wolf, or the evil witch, leaving them free to identify their more pleasing side with the fairy godmother or the brave woodcutter.

The importance of death and violence in traditional stories

We live in a culture that is uncomfortable with death. This is reflected in the stories we deem suitable, or unsuitable, to tell to children. In modern versions of traditional tales, death has been pushed out and violence watered down. No longer does the wolf eat the first two pigs, nor is he cooked for supper by the third.

This squeamishness comes from a tendency to take the stories too literally and from an adult discomfort with death and violence that is not shared by children.

If you think of the wolf in The Three Little Pigs, for example, as a real and endangered beautiful wild animal who is only trying to survive, you will understandably not want him dead at the end of the story. If, on the other hand, you see him as a metaphor, perhaps it is not so crucial that he survives. The wolf might stand for a child's destructive tendencies, or for hate or jealousy. It might have other meanings. The wolf 'dies' in the sense that these tendencies are resolved within the context of the story.

Similarly, the 'death' of the first little pigs can be seen, not literally, but as representing the need for a child to move on from a life with no demands, a carefree existence, and to accept the growing responsibilities of the older child. Like the third pig, the school-aged child must work hard. Letting go of an earlier stage of development is sad – it is like a little death. This is appropriate and such little sorrows prepare us for coping with the larger ones that life will inevitably bring.

If we take the sadness out of the story, we send children the worrying message that sadness is so awful that we, the adult telling the story, cannot bear to put it into words, let alone think about and experience it. Not mentioning a subject actually draws attention to it and magnifies it in a child's eyes.

The same is true of death. If we cannot bear to put death in our stories, if it is too awful even to say the word, then we increase children's anxieties about an important and natural subject. We also deprive them of the opportunity of thinking or talking about death in a safe place and in a calm environment. Telling stories that contain death means children can ask questions about it if they wish and implies that it is an acceptable topic for conversation.

Children can feel powerful emotions. They hate and sometimes they wish to destroy. These feelings are not abnormal and are only a problem when they are acted upon. Stories provide a safe outlet or channel for the normal and powerful emotions that are part of being human. Children are able to project their own desire to hurt others into a big bad wolf and then find relief when the wolf is destroyed at the end of the story. This reassures them that their own destructive feelings can be controlled and will not triumph in the end, and at the same time it satisfies their strong sense of justice.

For these reasons, when I tell traditional stories, I always keep the death and the violence in them, and I find that children love it. It does not frighten them – it frightens their teachers sometimes, but not the children, or at least not unpleasantly so. The fear they feel is a limited and safe fear, and children need to learn how to cope with fear in small doses without feeling overwhelmed. Fear is exciting, even a little enjoyable – why else would we watch horror films? Children enjoy being a little bit frightened, provided they feel otherwise safe and secure. Children also relish the destruction in stories because it resonates with their own destructive desires and tells them that these characters felt like that, too. They are not alone.

It is worth noting that I do not play up the death and the violence – I speak these parts of the story quietly and with restraint. It is not my aim to frighten young children unduly. However, neither do I shy away from stating the facts of death or violence in stories calmly and without using euphemisms.

Older children are rather different. I will build tension and startle a group of Year 6 children – they enjoy and are able to cope with a more robust storytelling style that might unsettle younger children. Clearly it is important to be sensitive to the needs of the audience – but not over-sensitive. Children are resilient and need to learn to cope with fear in small doses.

Traditional tales and older children

Traditional tales work metaphorically and like all works of art can mean very different things to different people. This means that a child may find the same tale useful and compelling at different ages and for very different reasons.

Bettelheim gives an example of a five-year-old girl, struggling with a rather distant mother, who found great consolation and help from Snow White. Usually, Snow White is seen as a story about puberty and the need to turn from the parents to the outside world and other relationships. This five-year-old, however, found her own problems reflected in and supported by the story.

I used a variety of children's stories and traditional tales with a group of teenaged girls I was working with. These girls were in local authority care and had all suffered neglect and abuse by adults. We were reading and rewriting stories within the context of a project on children's books. The girls related very strongly to Snow White, which can, at one level, be seen as a story about parental neglect and abuse, and they asked to hear the story repeatedly. The connection with their own backgrounds was not made explicit for them – that would have been intrusive and inappropriate in an educational setting. At times, however, the connection was so clear to the adults present that we found it deeply painful. I vividly recall a teenager drawing my attention to an illustration of Snow White running through the forest with her legs and arms scratched and bleeding. The girl's own arms were covered with self-inflicted wounds and the parallel was disturbing and vivid. Avoiding the story would have been much more comfortable, but it felt necessary for us as adults to endure the sadness and discomfort of this awareness to enable the girls to experience and identify with an essentially hopeful tale.

All of the girls clearly found working with this story, and others like it, a profoundly satisfying experience as well as one that motivated them to produce an unusually high level of academic work of their own.

Other stories that relate to puberty and which therefore might be appropriate to tell to older children are Rapunzel, Beauty and the Beast and the Queen Bee. It is not really important whether the hero or heroine is a boy or a girl – children can relate different aspects of themselves to different characters in the story.

You may feel that a group of older children would benefit from listening again to tales they heard when they were little. Perhaps they may have missed out on much experience of traditional tales, or perhaps they may be going through a stressful time as a group and you feel that they would be reassured and comforted by familiar tales.

If you wish to tell a story traditionally told to younger children to older ones, do so playfully and imaginatively. Invite Year 6 children to mind map what they can remember of The Three Billy Goats Gruff and then to retell it in small groups, comparing what was identical, what was similar and what was completely different about each group's retelling of the tale. (A mind map is a diagram combining words and pictures that puts ideas onto paper.)

Alternatively use the simpler stories to play games with. A listening game I use is one I call 'Three Pigs Plus'. The children have, first, to suggest several friends and a pet for each little pig. The aim is to have at least fifteen different characters in the story. Each child is then allocated one character, either a pig, a friend or a pet. With an average class size of thirty, that usually means there are two children for each character. I then tell the story and the children have to stand up and sit down every time their character is mentioned – faster than the other child with the same character. All the children have to stand up when I mention the word 'wolf'. Chaos but creative chaos!

All the traditional tales exist in different versions so it is entirely acceptable for the children to produce their own, writing alternative endings, adding or subtracting characters, writing it from a different viewpoint. They might research as many different versions of a single tale as they can find and then do one that is different again. There is a lovely book, *The Annotated Classic Fairy Tales* by Maria Tatar (2002), which gives good background information on all the classic tales and also tells you which parts the Victorian moralists thought unsuitable for children!

The meaning of traditional tales

I never explain to children what a story 'means'. Partly this is because it would be intrusive for the children – their private inner worlds are their affair and it is not for us to say why they enjoy a particular story or find it meaningful. It is also because we are quite likely to be wrong. We may think that John is perhaps finding The Three Billy Goats Gruff particularly satisfying because he is finding his brothers annoying and likes to imagine the troll eating them up and is busy projecting his aggression into the good old troll. And perhaps that is what is happening. On the other hand, perhaps he is fed up with being seven and likes to imagine what will happen when he is big enough to go out into the world and face trolls and bridges of his own. Or perhaps he's just enjoying the rhythm and the words! We don't know and certainly shouldn't ask him.

On the other hand, our wondering about why John relates so strongly to this particular story *is* helpful to him. The adult attempt to understand and see things from a child's point of view is an important part of the adult–child relationship and helps to contain anxiety and support healthy emotional development in the child. Noticing the importance of a particular story to a child may prompt us to make more opportunities available for them to hear or read it and also to provide play opportunities related to the story so that they can continue working on it in their imagination. We may also find ourselves thinking of similar stories with related themes that they may enjoy.

A third reason not to explain what a story 'means' is that when we impose our own meaning on a story we cut off other meanings. The child who hears that Hansel and Gretel is really a story about children worrying they may get lost, then feels that their own, entirely different, interpretation is wrong. You are an adult. You must be right. The child's own interpretation – perhaps its many interpretations – is then shut off and the story loses much of its usefulness and possibly much of its magic. The child's interpretations are not really conscious – they remain half noticed and sensed – mysterious and wonderful, and that is as it should be. Traditional tales are tales of wonder.

If you can think about the possible symbolic interpretations of stories, it will enhance their usefulness for the children you teach. Consider the ordinary struggles faced by all children: separation from parents; going out into the world; new siblings being born; sibling rivalry; fear of abandonment; bullying by older children; being misunderstood; feeling lost and helpless; the conflict of instant gratification versus responsibilities; rivalry with parents at puberty; growing sexual awareness. Then think about the tales that you know which might convey some of those struggles in metaphorical form. Telling children a rich variety of traditional tales throughout their early school careers means that the stories they need are never far away.

If you were telling stories to a single child you could rely on them to pick the story they most wanted to hear at any time, but a group is more complex. You might certainly let individual children pick the stories from time to time, perhaps a child who had been troubled or difficult that day might choose. Alternatively, you can make sure that as many tales as possible are told and available in as many different versions as possible and make story and storytelling a regular part of your classroom activities.

Also trust your own instincts and pick a story that seems appropriate to you. You are with the children all day and pick up an immense amount from them, much of it unconscious, about their emotional states. Your instincts will guide you to appropriate stories at appropriate times.

Storytelling suggestions

Play 'Three Pigs Plus' as a listening game for older juniors. Adapt other simple stories in the same way and let the children add the characters.

The Three Feathers is a less well-known tale by the Brothers Grimm. I tell it using three feathers as simple props.

The Three Feathers

Once upon a time a king had three sons. Two of the sons were clever and bold, but the third was such a simple lad that his brothers called him Dummy.

Now the king was old and knew that he must soon die, but he did not know which son should be king after him. So he called his sons together and said, 'Whoever brings me back the finest carpet in the land to lay at the foot of my throne, he shall be king after me.'

And he held up three feathers and blew, saying, 'Each of you shall follow a feather …'. One flew to the east and the first son followed that feather. One flew to the west and the second son followed that feather, but one feather just fell to the ground and stayed there. The brothers laughed at Dummy as they set off.

Dummy sat down, feeling sad. He looked at the feather and found that under it was a trap door. He lifted the door and found some steps going down, down into the ground. Dummy followed the steps, down, down into the ground and when he got to the bottom, he found – a huge green slimy frog.

He told the frog what he wanted and she gave him the most beautiful carpet in the world to lay at the foot of the throne. Dummy took it to the king who said, 'Now, you must be king after me.'

But the other brothers, who had brought back two, tatty, tired rugs, moaned and scolded and whinged SO much that the king said, 'Very well, there shall be another test. Whoever brings me back a beautiful ring to place upon my finger, he shall be king after me.' And he held up three feathers and blew, saying, 'Each of you shall follow a feather …'. One flew to the east and the first son followed that feather. One flew to the west and the second son followed that feather, but one feather just fell to the ground and stayed there. The brothers laughed at Dummy as they set off once more.

This time, Dummy didn't feel sad at all. He opened the trap door and followed the steps down, down into the ground to where the huge green slimy frog was waiting for him. He told her what he wanted and she gave him a beautiful ring to place upon the king's finger. Dummy took it to the king who said, 'Now you must be king after me.'

But the other brothers, who had brought back two tatty, rusty iron rings, moaned and scolded and whinged SO much that the king said, 'Very well, there shall be one more test. Whoever brings back the most beautiful woman to be his bride shall be king after me.' And he held up three feathers and blew, saying, 'Each of you shall follow a feather ...'. One flew to the east and the first son followed that feather. One flew to the west and the second son followed that feather, but one feather just fell to the ground and stayed there. The brothers laughed at Dummy as they set off a third time.

At once, Dummy opened the trap door and followed the steps down, down into the ground to where the huge green slimy frog was waiting for him. He told her what he wanted and she gave him a tiny carriage made of a carrot, pulled by six tiny mice. Dummy looked at it in dismay and asked the frog what he was to do with it. She called to a little frog standing nearby and told Dummy to put the little frog in the carriage. Dummy did so and at once, the little frog turned into the most beautiful woman he had ever seen.

When he took her to the king, he said, 'Now you must be king after me.' Now, the other brothers had bribed the first women they met to come back with them and, though they were pretty, they were cross and bad tempered. But when the brothers heard what the king said they moaned and scolded and whinged SO much that the king sighed and said, 'Very well, one last test. The bride who jumps through the golden ring, hanging over my throne, her husband shall be king after me.'

Well, the cross, bad-tempered women the brothers had found refused to so much as try to jump through the ring. But Dummy's beautiful bride leapt lightly and gracefully through the ring just as the king had said.

Dummy became king and ruled wisely and well, while the brothers married their bad-tempered women who moaned and scolded and whinged at their husbands and, for all I know, they're still moaning now.

4.

Creating Unique Stories

You create a unique story each time you tell, as opposed to read aloud, a story. No two retellings are ever quite the same. A word changes here, an emphasis is different there. The storyteller responds unconsciously to the messages and signals sent by the audience and to her own feelings and mood at that moment, to create a unique event. If you told The Three Little Pigs twice in quick succession, the second retelling would be different, however subtly, from the first.

Creating stories as a teacher

You can also, once you become familiar with telling traditional stories, begin to branch out and create new stories for your class. There are different models that you can use to create unique stories. One is to think of an element, out of earth, air, fire or water. If you choose fire, for example, you would then choose a character that fits that element. A magical salamander, for example, that lives in fire, or a fire-breathing dragon. Or perhaps just an animal from a hot country, like a lizard. Then you would think of a fiery setting for your creature – an oven, a volcano, a desert or a living room with a fire on a winter's day. Think next of a fiery object for your story, a flaming arrow, or a lightning bolt, or a ring that has magic writing revealed in the fire (you can borrow ideas from famous authors, too!).

Then there could be a problem or difficulty to overcome and a helping character. Finally, there is the solution to the difficulty and the ending.

If you want to explore making up stories for yourself, you could also experiment with suiting your story to the mood of the children. Choose fiery stories for example on hot, bad-tempered days, or on powerful, energetic days – it is another way that you can convey your understanding of the children and help them to articulate emotions rather than acting them out.

Another model, quoted by Molly Salans in her book, *Storytelling with Children in Crisis*, uses six elements for creating stories. She uses a good, a bad and a helping character, which can be animals or people, plus a time and a place and a magical object (Salans 2004, p.14). She uses stories to work with troubled children and the children create the stories for themselves. However, there is no reason you should not use this model to create stories to tell to the children you teach.

Collective stories

Alternatively, of course, you can work with a group or class of children to create a story together. So often, as teachers, we ask children to make up stories as individuals. However, groups are very creative, and a story that is produced by a group will express the life and mood of that group in a way that is distinct from a story produced by an individual. In addition, as teachers, we rarely work alongside the children. We give them work to do but it is less common for them to see us writing or reading or being creative ourselves. You can be an active participant in the process of making a collective story, a part of the group, and model for the children a willingness to risk the vulnerability of being creative. You can also relax and let them see you enjoying being creative and throwing your ideas into the melting pot alongside theirs.

A story that the class has created then becomes a record of your life together, a snapshot that potentially reveals more to the thoughtful reader or listener than any photo could possibly do.

You could scribe such collective stories for the children. It would be good to do this by hand. In this age of computers and easy printing software, children are in danger of never seeing adults writing anything down by hand. Your handwriting expresses your personality in a way that print can never do, and you show great respect for the children's story if you take the time to carefully write it out on large card to make into a simple book. You may not consider your handwriting to be a work of art, but the children will not mind this – they will appreciate the work and care that you have shown though usually they may not express this.

The children can then enjoy illustrating the book and will treasure it as something they have all had a part in creating.

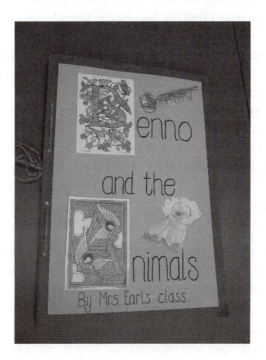

A handwritten record of a version of Benno and the Beasts composed and illustrated by Mrs Earl's class at Riddings Infant School.

Turning events into stories

As you and the children grow in confidence as storytellers, you will find you can turn real events into stories. We all do this, of course. Every teacher has, at some time, if not every day, gone into the staff room with a funny story of something that has just happened in class.

You can do this with the children themselves, too. Here is an example of a story I made up with my son after we found our cat sitting in the – empty – guinea pig cage.

Harry and the Guinea Pigs' Hutch

Last night, after supper, we decided to get the guinea pigs out.

We shut Freyja, our little cat, in the kitchen.

We shut our dog, Bonnie, in the boys' bedroom.

But we couldn't find our biggest cat, Harry!

We put the guinea pigs in a box and carried them upstairs. We took the guinea pigs out and they ran around in the hall. When we tried to catch them again, Emma climbed up Daddy's trouser leg!

What a silly pig!

When we caught them, Emily hid in Annwyn's hair.

What a silly pig!

We had to stroke them and cuddle them to calm them down.

We put them back in the box and me and Mummy took them downstairs to the cellar. Then we found Harry! He was sitting in the guinea pigs' hutch!!!!

What a silly cat!

We turned this incident into a story together and then he told it to me and I told it back to him. The last process was to type it up for him and to get his brother to do some funny pictures to go with it.

You will notice the storytelling elements of simple sentences, repetition and a gradual build up to the final event.

You can really take any incident and turn it into a story in this way and, again, keep a file of such stories. This kind of story does not have to be technically wonderful. It is just you putting the day, or an incident, into words for the children. If appropriate, make it funny. Clearly you would never laugh at the children themselves or at what they do or say, but you can certainly laugh at yourself and your mistakes or at things that go wrong. Becoming a story makes an event more memorable – it becomes a treasured memory, something to store up against the hard times.

You can include difficult events too, if you wish, but keep the balance positive and always end on a positive note. This kind of story need not ignore the difficult times; indeed if you ignore difficult events or emotions completely and don't refer to them it can increase children's anxieties about them. Putting such occasions gently into a story and balancing them with the good things that happened in the day can, on the other hand, reduce children's anxieties about what might have felt uncomfortable at the time. It can also teach the valuable lesson of putting events in perspective – even the very worst days have some good parts in them.

You show the children that you, their teacher, can cope with and think about anger or conflicts and that they don't stop you noticing the good things that happen, too.

You might tell a story of A Mixed Sort of Day which started badly: 'Tuesday started badly! First, my car broke down on the way to work and I was in a bad mood. Then everyone was a bit noisy and my mood got even worse. Then someone dropped paint all over the floor and I went BALLISTIC. Oh dear!'

You can use this technique to gently comment on what happened and to show the children that difficult emotions can be thought about, survived and moved on from. Use humour if you can, make your own part in it funny and make it clear that losing your temper is something you regret but that you are human too, which is why it happens. Always move on to and concentrate on the positive things. 'After that, things got better. John very kindly cleared up the paint for me. I decided spilled paint was not THAT important and I stopped shouting. When I stopped shouting, oddly enough, everyone else quietened down too and got on with their work! It got better. All the children worked really hard and all sorts of good work was done…It turned into a good day after all!'

Everyone knows the morning was difficult and that you felt angry. Leaving that part out of your story can increase the children's anxiety – they can think anger is too awful to put into words. Articulating the 'bad bits' as well as the 'good bits' – and a story is a safe way of doing this – tells all the children that you are no longer angry and can even find the positive element, or the humour within the event to look back upon and remember.

I would not record such stories, however. Articulating them is important, but we want to teach children to dwell on the positive aspects of life, so once such a story has been told it can be quietly forgotten.

Putting children into stories

One way you can show children a little special attention is by putting them into your stories. I have done this with a Bob Hartman story called The Big Soft Fluffy Bed (Hartman 2002). I tell the children I'd like to 'borrow' a name for the story and ask for a volunteer. Then I tell the story inserting the child's name at the appropriate points.

When I asked a group of children I had worked with periodically over a year what they had enjoyed most about the story work we had done, many of them chose the time I had used Ethan's name to tell a story. Not only Ethan, but many of the other children, too, found that occasion meaningful and exciting.

You might pick a child who you feel could do with feeling special that day and use their name. Alternatively, if you are struggling to build a positive relationship with a particular child, choose them. It will help to assure the child that you notice and think about them. Some children struggle to believe that their teacher cares about them in a positive way and this kind of activity is one more way of reassuring them and building their trust.

Unfinished tales

A lovely technique for helping children take the first steps towards creating their own, unique story, is to ask them to help you complete a story before you tell it. This builds on the technique used to retell Little Red Riding Hood, where children's suggestions for what to put in the basket are included in the story. It can be used for most stories but some lend themselves to it more than others.

One story I have done this with frequently is a tale I call Benno and the Beasts. It is based on a story called St Benno and the Frog, found in an old book by Helen Waddell (1934). In the original, the saint meets a frog in a marsh and tells it to be quiet in case it disturbs his prayers. Later, he regrets this, in case God was enjoying listening to the sound of the frog.

I invite children to think of different animals for the saint to meet and different places for him to meet them. I then tell them the story incorporating their own ideas. It is a most effective way of involving children in the art of creating stories and they love hearing their ideas used.

Social stories

Social stories are a particular kind of unique story that are increasingly used with children with special needs, particularly autism. Developed by Carol Gray in America, the stories are written accounts of specific situations that a child finds difficult (Gray 1994). They contain *descriptive* sentences, information about what is happening, who is involved, what they are doing and why. They also contain *perspective* sentences, which describe the reactions and feelings of the people involved. Lastly, they may contain *directive* sentences which describe, in positive terms, what the child can try to do in the given situation. Carol Rowe (1999) describes one highly effective use of a social story to help a boy with Asperger's syndrome change his behaviour at lunch times. His story helped him eat calmly alongside other children instead of shouting at them to be quiet and leaving much of his own lunch.

Rowe speculates that the effectiveness of this story approach owes much to the communication of background knowledge which increases a child's understanding of a situation and therefore their ability to respond appropriately.

It may also be that the story acts as a way of containing a child's anxiety about a certain situation and his or her own part in it. Increased knowledge usually serves to reduce anxiety so this may be an important element in why social stories work.

Another reason such stories may work is that they are an indirect teaching method, and children may be able to assimilate and respond to information more readily when it is presented in an indirect form, especially when there is anxiety attached to the subject being taught.

I used a 'story' approach with a young boy with an autistic spectrum disorder (ASD) who was feeling a considerable degree of anxiety about his future and who had decided that he needed to move on to 'nursery'. The boy had attended a mainstream nursery and was now in a specialist infant unit for children with ASD attached to a mainstream primary school. He was in Year 1 and his future was uncertain. He had decided for himself that after he had finished Year 1 he needed to go back to the nursery. The adults around him explained that this was not possible, but he was adamant and grew distressed if people insisted that this could not happen.

I put together a collection of photographs showing Peter at different stages of development, from birth to his current six years and wrote a simple story with the refrain, 'and then he got bigger'. At each age I wrote about what he was achieving, so 'When Peter was one he could walk and play with bricks; when Peter was two he liked to play with his train set ... etc. The page where he was four contained a reference to him attending nursery and the story ended with an exclamatory 'and he's STILL getting bigger!'. The story was written up in a little book and read with him as often as he wished. He loved it and his anxious insistence that he move on to nursery stopped completely. Through the story he had been able to accept the concept of growing up and moving on and to realise that nursery had been a stage in his development that he had to let go of.

Such stories could be used for many children, not only those with ASDs. Positive stories affirm children and respect their independence as learners. They do not have to accept what is being presented to them in the story – they can choose. This is empowering for children and if they do decide to accept the information presented in the story, it will almost certainly be learned more fully because of the element of choice involved.

Storytelling suggestions

Think of an incident from the previous week and turn it into a simple story to tell the children. You could start off 'I thought I'd tell you the story of the day when Mrs Eades was so busy she forgot to send her class out to play!'

Retell Benno and the Beasts with the children, but ask them for their own ideas for animals, sounds and habitats. Then tell it, using their ideas and asking them to supply the sound effects.

Benno and the Beasts

Once, long ago, there lived a holy man, a monk called Benno. And Benno liked to go for walks outside beneath the sky and to talk, as he walked, to God who is good at listening.

One day, as Benno was walking and talking and praying, he came to a muddy marshland and he heard a frog croaking.

'Ribbit, ribbit', went the frog. Benno stopped. 'SHUT UP,' shouted Benno, 'I can't hear myself pray!' And the frog shut up.

Benno carried on walking and talking and praying, until he came to a dense green forest and he heard a bird singing. Benno stopped again.

'Cheep, cheep', went the bird. 'SHUT UP,' shouted Benno, 'I can't hear myself pray!' And the bird shut up.

Benno carried on walking and talking and praying, until he came to a high rocky mountain and he heard a wolf, howling.

'Oowwwooo', went the wolf. 'SHUT UP,' shouted Benno, 'I can't hear myself pray!' And the wolf shut up.

Benno carried on walking and talking and praying, until he came to a deep wide lake and he heard a fish, splashing.

'Splish, splash', went the fish. 'SHUT UP,' shouted Benno, 'I can't hear myself pray!' And the fish shut up.

Suddenly, Benno had a terrible thought. What if God liked listening to the frog croaking and the bird singing and the wolf howling and the fish splashing MORE than he liked listening to Benno's prayers?

Benno turned and rushed back to the deep wide lake. 'I'm sorry,' he yelled, to the fish, 'splash all you like,' so the fish started splashing.

He rushed back to the high rocky mountain. 'I'm sorry,' he yelled to the wolf, 'howl all you like,' so the wolf started howling. He rushed back to the dense green forest. 'I'm sorry,' he yelled to the bird, 'sing all you like,' so the bird started singing. He rushed back to the muddy marsh. 'I'm sorry,' he yelled to the frog, 'croak all you like,' so the frog started croaking.

And Benno listened to the splashing of the fish, and the howling of the wolf and the singing of the bird and the croaking of the frog and he wondered why he had never noticed before how beautiful they sounded. And he added his own prayers to theirs. And God, who is good at listening, listened to it all, and smiled.

5.

Children as Storytellers

People were telling stories long before writing was invented, so it is slightly paradoxical that children are expected to write stories before they have learned how to tell them. To an extent, children are natural storytellers – they come to school bursting with news about their weekend that they want to share with you, or they come in from playtime full of the story of what happened in the playground. These accounts are their first stories and provide a foundation for both anecdotal writing and accounts of real life and also for the move to writing and telling fictional or fantastic stories.

It is important to provide space for this kind of anecdotal storytelling because it is when children are listened to and their stories are valued that they gain confidence and proficiency in the art of speaking. A teacher may not always feel they have the time to devote to listening to children in this way, but it is worth remembering that such conversations are not things that happen before or after the lesson – they are an essential part of the lesson itself. If you cannot give a coherent spoken account of what happened to you over the weekend, you will not be able to write one down either.

The exception to this, and there is always an exception, is the shy or introverted child who comes to life on paper. For them, writing down their thoughts and ideas will always be easier than talking about them. For such children, the ability to express themselves verbally, though more challenging, may be facilitated by writing things down first of all. Either reading aloud their stories or talking about them after they have been written may provide them with the confidence to communicate verbally, either one to one or in a group.

You could legitimately spend time with the children listening to one or two of their accounts of the weekend and thinking about what makes a 'story' effective. Could they identify the features that made Joe's account of his granddad's eightieth birthday cake catching on fire so exciting? Is there anything Joe could have done to make the account even more exciting? Is it permissible for Joe to exaggerate or adapt his story to make it more exciting? Or not?

Children telling traditional tales

A natural development from telling anecdotal stories is for children to tell traditional tales that they already know well.

Guidance from a teacher will be necessary when it comes to choosing which story to tell. When starting out as a teller of traditional tales it is important to begin with something simple, and while children may love Sleeping Beauty and Cinderella they are quite complex stories and not easy to tell well.

Good stories to start with are The Three Little Pigs, The Three Billy Goats Gruff or Little Red Riding Hood. They all have a simple structure and a lot of repetition of well-known phrases that can scaffold the children's first storytelling efforts.

The teacher may need to exercise the use of the veto on more complex stories; however, it is still important for children to make choices. An effective way of doing this is to ask the children for their suggestions about stories they may wish to tell. Explain why you are not going to write down the more complicated stories and ask if they can think of simpler ones. Then you ask them to vote. I give the children star-shaped cards and ask them to place them on the story of their choice. This works with children as young as Year 1 or 2. Reception children I would ask to choose from two possibilities only.

All of the children then work on the chosen story. The advantage of them all learning to tell the same story is that they learn, from experience, that different people tell stories in different ways – even if it is the same story. It also provides reinforcement of the story, allows them to observe and learn from one another's creative solutions and gives them an opportunity to comment positively on other children's versions of a familiar tale.

The first thing I do during this activity is to mind map (see p.41 for explanation) the story with the children and to build up a picture of what they remember about it. Then I tell them the story myself using a story box and simple props. After a minute's silent thinking time, we then go back to the mind map to see what they need to add, if anything.

Older children can work in pairs or threes and choose which story to tell. They can also produce their own mind map of 'everything they can remember about the story'. This brings the story to the front of their minds before they attempt to put it into words.

The children then work in small groups to begin to actually tell the story. Groups of three or four work well, though reception or Year 1 children might work in pairs instead. Pairs would also be worth using if a class of children of any age had particularly poor listening and social skills.

Children working together to tell a traditional tale using a story box.

Adapting the story box technique, I give children an empty box, a cloth to tell the story on and a scarf. Then I ask them to choose props to tell the story. Using props is a good technique to use to start telling stories, for children or for adults. They provide visual and kinaesthetic prompts for the memory and seem to carry the story forward and alleviate anxiety, however reticent or shy the novice storyteller.

With children, we look first at the props I used to tell the story that they have chosen and discuss the fact that the wolf was not, in fact, a wolf – it was a small piece of wood which was symbolising the wolf in the story. For younger children this provides a concrete introduction to the use of symbol and metaphor. We discuss the fact that I chose which props to use and which characters or objects to symbolise. I might have used props for the three pigs and their houses, but not for the people they met or the wolf, for example. Another time, I might use different props and make different choices. The children find it fascinating that I can tell the story using props but not use a prop for a central character – they begin to realise the power of their own imaginations to supply what is left out.

The children, working in their groups, then need to decide together which characters and objects in the story are going to have props and what the props should be. I offer them a variety of things to choose from – pebbles, glass beads, feathers, pipe cleaners, wooden bricks. I keep the props as neutral as possible – I feel it stretches the imagination that much further to use a glass bead as a wolf or as Little Red Riding Hood rather than a plastic person for example. I also place a limit on the number of props they can use – I usually tell them no more than ten objects. This limit stretches the children creatively since they have to adapt and make decisions about what to symbolise and what not to symbolise. It also stretches their social skills since decisions must be made collectively.

Storytelling and social skills

Children of all ages find this kind of co-operative work highly challenging. The need to give and take, to let others make choices, to listen to each others' ideas are all very difficult. Older children do not necessarily find it any easier than younger ones – Years 5 and 6 can find listening to one another just as challenging as Years 1 and 2. However, the need and desire to tell the story does provide a high incentive to reach an agreement about what is going to be used and how the story will be told. As an added incentive I may tell children they are going to have a certain time to learn to tell the story and then they will be asked to tell it to the other groups.

If an adult is available to model negotiation and to facilitate discussion where personalities clash, that is valuable. For this reason you might wish to consider storytelling as an activity for a section of a class rather than a whole class. On the other hand, it does also work as a whole class activity.

Many children do not know how to work in teams. Giving them explicit guidance on how to encourage each other is important. I ask children to use as many positive comments as they can and you might even list them:

- That's a good idea.

- Well done.

- Good start.

- I like the way you said that.

It may seem obvious to us, but a surprising number of children never say anything positive to one another and if they are to work in a team, as storytellers, good communication like this is essential. The aim is that everyone in the group should be happy and should be appreciative of the others' contributions.

Playing with the story

Once the children have chosen which props to use, they need to work out how to use them as they tell the story, when to get them out of the box, which words to use at which points. To begin with, children can get so excited about moving the props around the cloth that they forget to speak, but gradually, as they calm down and prompt one another, the story itself comes to the fore and the props cease to dominate their attention in quite the same way. It is worthwhile allowing them a certain amount of 'playing' time. Some older children seem almost to have forgotten how to play and find this activity as valuable as younger ones. All children will find that this play is creative and allows rich ideas to emerge.

During this time of playing with the story, the children need to ensure that they can recall all of the essential parts – this means they have to exercise judgement over just what is essential and what is not. They also have to decide on their choice of words.

The next step is for each group of children to be given one scarf – the storytelling scarf. Only the person wearing the scarf is allowed to speak or move the props on the cloth. This is a simple technique that gives quieter children permission to assert themselves with their peers in a way they might not otherwise do. Again, the children have to negotiate and agree who starts the story, how much of the story each person tells and when to hand the scarf on. Peer pressure is useful here since children's innate sense of fair play will work to discourage the dominant group members from 'hogging the limelight' for too long.

Let the children tell the story through a few times and encourage them to help one another to remember the story and to think of creative ways of telling it. You might insist that they keep the same order and the same section of the story each time so that they are able to gain familiarity and fluency within their section of the story. Also point out to the groups that when they are not actually speaking they still have a vital role to play – that of listening to and supporting the person wearing the scarf at that moment. Emphasise again the need to encourage, to whisper 'well done' at hand-over points, to smile at each other.

Every storyteller needs an audience and when the children have had a chance to practise their stories they can tell them to the other groups who have been engaged in the same activity.

Positive listening

Relationships, whether between friends or family members, flourish when the people involved take the time to value and affirm each other. Some children do not naturally make positive comments to one another and it is a vital social skill that can be taught in the context of group story-telling.

The first step in positive listening is for the children to listen to you tell a story and to remember, and comment on, what they liked. Younger children focus on which part of the story they liked. Older children, with encouragement, may focus more on technique, on how the story was told and what they considered effective. They are asked to notice what went well so that they can build on it in their own storytelling practice.

This is a variant on an activity I call 'WWW – What Went Well'. I write WWW in the middle of a sheet of paper and then write their comments around it.

When they have been working together in a group telling stories, they can then do WWW cards for each other. Each child has a card with WWW and their name written in the middle. The other children in the group, and any adult observers, write on the card what they think that child did well during the activity.

When children have listened to another group tell a story, they can fill out WWW cards for them, too. Discourage criticism of technique. Children learn best in this situation from having their strengths appreciated and pointed out to them so that they can build on them. The positive comments need to be as specific as possible. To begin with, younger children especially tend to mirror the comments they have heard adults make and need to be helped to think of what it was they *really* liked.

Also discourage phrases like 'that was wonderful' – such overblown praise is fairly meaningless. It is far more effective to say, 'I liked the way you had white glass beads in the river as bones of people the troll had eaten before' or 'I loved the really scary voice you used for the wolf when he tried to eat Little Red Riding Hood'. Giving specific and appropriate praise is an invaluable skill and the storytelling setting is a good one in which to practise it. On the card you might simply write 'imaginative use of props' but tell them specifically what it was you noticed.

Group storytelling of this kind is a very effective social and creative activity. Children can develop, very rapidly, from a group of competing, squabbling individuals into a team of people working together to tell a story effectively and imaginatively, supporting and helping each other.

It is worth remembering, too, that this kind of work brings a feeling of great personal satisfaction to children. The children are in charge – it is their story. I have seen quiet children, not normally seen as gifted academically, sit up straighter when given the story scarf and tell a story with confidence, creativity and immense pride. The sense of being in control is one that some children experience all too rarely. It contributes greatly to children's growing resilience and is a protective factor against stressful life events (Fonagy *et al.* 1994, p.232).

Story tennis

Story tennis is a storytelling game that really puts pressure on the children to listen to one another and to carry a story forward rapidly. It builds on the storytelling method above, using props and a scarf but you limit the time each child is wearing the scarf by ringing a bell after two minutes. When they hear the bell, the child with the scarf must stop the story wherever they have got up to and pass the scarf to the next child. That child must continue telling the story *exactly* where the last child stopped. If they have not been listening, they cannot continue the story.

If the child with the scarf finishes the story in their two minutes, they can start it again and the cycle can continue. Older children might choose a different story and start that one instead. This activity is as long as a piece of string since the children will find themselves telling new parts of the story each time the scarf reaches them. Older children will enjoy the challenge of seeing how many stories they can get through and how well they can remember them.

Children creating stories for themselves

The models described for teachers to use to compose unique stories can also be used with children to help them make up unique stories for themselves. Be careful to make sure that the process of composing a story is made quite distinct from the process of writing that story out. Writing is a very different task from making up a story and one that can seriously inhibit children's imaginations or willingness to be creative. If you are worried about how to spell 'wolf' you will avoid putting that wicked, resonant, powerful character into your story and make do with a 'dog' instead because you know how to spell it. It is worth remembering that Milton did not 'write' 'Paradise Lost'. He couldn't. He was blind and Braille had not yet been invented. He composed it and someone else wrote it down for him.

When it comes to composing unique stories, let children explore other methods besides pencil or paper. First, of course, a good story should be told, orally. If it is going to work well, a story needs to be memorable without having to be written down. Encourage the children to tell one another their stories and to remember them, so that they can retell them in broadly the same way on more than one occasion. This will have the advantage of making sure that the story makes sense, at least to the teller, and is not too complicated.

Children could use props such as those described above, and a story box to make up and tell a unique story, either individually or in groups. Ask them to choose ten props without giving them any other instruction. Then ask them to make up a story that uses every single prop they have chosen. The props themselves will provide the ideas for the story. Encourage them to think about:

- where the story is set
- how many characters there are
- if there is a hero and a villain
- what problem there is to overcome
- who helps the hero
- what happens at the end.

Or, use single objects to inspire stories. An interesting vase, a pebble, a painting can all be used as starting points for oral stories:

- Who made it?
- Who found it?
- Where?
- When?
- Is it magic?
- How does the magic work?
- How might the magic go wrong?
- What would fix it?

Children could draw stories instead of writing them down. You can use different methods for this. One way is to depict a story as a map, drawing the essential scenes on a single sheet of paper and then using words to string them together. A similar technique is to draw a story as a journey with a beginning, three main hills (or events) to climb, and an end. A third would be to use a story 'wand', a thin stick with small squares of paper (or Post-it notes) stuck on. On each Post-it they would draw a scene from the story. It would then be a relatively simple task to use words to join the scenes together. Such drawings, it is important to remember, are not meant as works of art. They are simply aids for the memory – don't let the children get distracted by putting huge effort into their drawings at this stage.

Simple books can be made from a sheet of A3 paper. Fold it in four, snip along the closed edge and fix the 'spine'. You should have eight sides on which to create a story.

A long sheet of wallpaper on the floor could be decorated, at random, by the children. They could draw characters and scenery as they wish. Then the challenge would be to make up a story that linked the pictures they had drawn. An interesting class story would evolve from such an activity.

Freed from anxiety about writing, children can flourish as authors and composers of stories. Children who struggle with literacy or who have learning difficulties can shine as imaginative and creative thinkers. This kind of work does not really require differentiation because it already works on many levels and the children will explore and work in the way that suits their learning needs – their stories will reflect their interests, concerns, hopes and ambitions.

Storytelling suggestion

This is a simple version of The Three Little Pigs that children can base their own versions upon. You can tell it with no props at all or with a story box. The children can then choose their own props to retell it.

The Three Little Pigs

Once upon a time, there lived a mother pig and her three little pigs. The day came when the little pigs grew too big to live at home, so their mother sent them out into the world to seek their fortunes.

The first little pig met a man carrying a bundle of straw. 'May I have some straw', said the pig, 'to build myself a house?'

'Of course,' said the man, and he gave the first little pig some straw.

The little pig built his house quickly and easily and then spent the rest of the day playing and dancing in the sun. But that evening, who should come along but the big bad wolf? The little pig ran into his straw house and shut the door.

The wolf knocked at the door, saying, 'Little pig, little pig, let me come in.'

'No,' said the pig, 'not by the hair on my chinny chin chin, I will NOT let you come in.'

'Then I'll huff and I'll puff and I'll blow your house in,' said the wolf. And he huffed and he puffed and he blew the house of straw down and ate up the first little pig.

The second little pig met a man carrying a bundle of sticks. 'May I have some sticks', said the pig, 'to build myself a house?'

'Of course,' said the man, and he gave the second little pig some sticks.

The little pig built his house quickly and easily and then spent the rest of the day playing in the sun. But that evening, who should come along but the big bad wolf?

The little pig ran into his house of sticks and shut the door. The wolf knocked at the door, saying, 'Little pig, little pig, let me come in.'

'No,' said the pig, 'not by the hair on my chinny chin chin, I will NOT let you come in.'

'Then I'll huff and I'll puff and I'll blow your house in,' said the wolf.

And he huffed and he puffed and he blew the house of straw down and ate up the second little pig.

The third little pig met a man carrying a bundle of bricks. 'May I have some bricks', said the pig, 'to build myself a house?'

'Of course,' said the man, and he gave the third little pig some bricks.

The third little pig worked hard all day, building a good, strong house of bricks. He had no time to play. He had just finished when who should come along but the big bad wolf? The little pig ran into his house of bricks and shut the door. The wolf knocked at the door, saying, 'Little pig, little pig, let me come in.'

'No,' said the pig, 'not by the hair on my chinny chin chin, I will NOT let you come in.'

'Then I'll huff and I'll puff and I'll blow your house in,' said the wolf.

And he huffed and he puffed, and he huffed and he puffed, and he huffed and he puffed till he could huff and puff no more, but the house of bricks would NOT fall down. It was too strong!

The wolf was VERY angry. So he climbed up the drain pipe and along the roof and peered down the chimney.

'I'm coming to eat you up!' called the wolf, getting ready to jump. But the third little pig was too clever for him. He took the lid off the cooking pot on the fire and when the wolf jumped down he landed in the pot with a great big splash! The pig put the lid back on and cooked that wicked wolf for his supper. And he lived happily ever after, safe and snug in his house of bricks.

6

Stories and Thinking Skills

Listening to stories and thinking skills

Listening to a story well told engages a child's thinking capacity. The need to provide detail, to imagine the scene, to empathise with the motives and the feelings of the characters involved, all exercises a child's ability to think and reason.

There are ways of following up stories that extend this capacity to reason and capitalise on the power of story to evoke and engage a child's emotions as well as their intellect.

Following a story with silence is important. This is vital thinking time and allows the images, ideas and emotions of the story to sink in and make connections with the child's previous knowledge and experience. There are different ways of following the silence that can develop thinking skills.

Philosophy for children

Philosophy for children is an approach to dialogue and thinking with children which has been used for many years but which is now becoming more widely known. It involves children engaging in open-ended, respectful discussion with one another about a topic that is of interest to them. It is challenging for teachers because the teacher facilitates but does not guide the discussion, nor do they tell children the answers to the questions they are discussing.

It is an excellent approach with which to follow a story. Philosophical discussion can allow children to explore profound issues of life and death, growing up, loving and hating. *Children as Philosophers* by Joanna Haynes (Haynes 2002) is a good introduction, and there is a charity called SAPERE which promotes philosophy and can provide training for teachers (see Appendix 2).

A philosophy session

After a story and some thinking time, older children may be asked to think of questions they want to discuss. Younger children take a while to grasp this idea – you may need to turn statements they make into questions until they learn how to do it for themselves. They can then explore a topic and develop it, learn to listen to each other as well as to a teacher and to think through the implications of their ideas.

Familiar stories provide a useful starting point for discussion. Using The Three Little Pigs some children in Year 2 raised the question of why the third little pig had built in brick. One lad suggested it was because he had some sense. Another, clearly noticing that the pig had overlooked a design flaw, asked why he hadn't bricked up the chimney. A third pointed out that if the chimney was bricked up, the smoke would have nowhere to escape from and this led another to suggest a solution to the problem, which was to leave a tiny hole for the smoke to escape. The problem then, it was suggested by these six-year-old philosophers, would be that the tail of the wolf might fall down the hole. That, however, was then seen to be an advantage, not a problem, as the tail might catch light from the fire below, the wolf be incinerated and the third little pig's troubles would be over.

Philosophy and emotional development

In the example above, the children were exploring logic and causation with admirable skill. On other occasions, more emotional issues may be raised. The questions the children suggest will be those that are important to them and they may raise issues that touch them directly. I prefer this method of working on difficult issues, which is indirect, to a more direct approach. I feel concern that otherwise, unless teachers are very careful, difficult and painful topics might be raised that cannot then be fully contained and dealt with in the lesson, either because a teacher lacks experience of working with these subjects or simply through lack of time.

Discussion that centres on a story allows topics to be raised in a safe and indirect way that does not require children to expose their inner selves – they are talking about the characters in a story, not themselves. If children wish to make connections to their own experience they may but personally I would never invite this in a group context.

Stories, because they work through metaphor, let children discuss difficult issues second, not first, hand. This is safer, less exposing, and leaves children feeling altogether less vulnerable than direct discussion of, for example, the death or loss of a close relative. At the same time, the emotions that might attend such an event may be thought about in a safe way, contained and supported by the story itself.

To give an example, after I had told The Three Little Pigs to a group of Year 1 children, a five-year-old boy wondered why the mother had made the pigs leave home. He then suggested it might be because she was expecting more piglets and there was therefore no room for the three in our story. This boy was raising quite a common fear of children of about this age, that mother might have more children who might supplant him. It is probably not a conscious fear but is no less powerful for that and it is possible that this, or a related anxiety, was behind the child's question.

We were able, as a group, to think calmly about his question. We didn't hide from the sadness of the idea and I didn't dismiss it with an 'oh that would never happen' – I wrote it down alongside the other questions and took it seriously. I also did not, of course, relate the question to the child or wonder why he had asked it. That would have invaded his privacy. Later I discovered that there were difficulties at home and that this child's parents subsequently separated. Through our discussion of The Three Little Pigs this child was able, I think, to express some of the anxieties he was feeling in a safe way.

Thinking about such hypothetical questions and keeping them completely hypothetical lets the questions be thought about and defuses anxiety. Making them personal would be painful, scary and inappropriate.

Another child wondered why the mother did not ask the pigs to build her a larger house if they had grown too big for the existing one. To this there were various responses. One child suggested that the mother might have sent the pigs out into the world because she was tired of them. Another said that she might not have been able to afford to keep them. Children here may have been expressing their doubts and anxieties about their own situations – I don't know, but it is possible. Children do worry whether their parents (even the most loving parents) will always love them or whether, if the child is too naughty, the parent will finally reject him or her. These fears may not be based in reality at all, but they are very real fears all the same and are not uncommon.

Another child raised the more positive view that the mother pig might have wanted her children to live in the countryside (this school was in an urban area).

These children were raising the issues that were foremost in their minds and finding relief for the ordinary anxieties of childhood. At the same time, they were extending their ability to engage in reasoned conversation, to consider questions and suggest solutions to problems and to explore a character's possible emotions and motivations. All of this will allow children to deal a little better with anxieties and to think a little more about fears that might otherwise remain, literally, 'unthinkable'.

To raise many of these issues directly with children – 'who worries their mum might have more babies and not want them anymore?' would of course be inappropriate and potentially harmful. To tell the Three Little Pigs and let children think about it and ask questions about it, is both appropriate academically and emotionally satisfying. It also simultaneously stimulates and supports the child's capacity to reason and reflect.

Using different versions of popular stories

The popular versions of traditional tales that have come down to us are only particular versions of the many similar oral tales that were once told. Maria Tatar's book, *The Annotated Classic Fairy Tales* (2002), is excellent for finding out about alternative endings, different characters and the background to the classic fairy tales. Discovering that the stories we tell have different versions can be liberating for children in their own creative work. They realise that individual storytellers, over the years, made their own changes to stories and that this ability to change elements is an important part of the creative process – it is all right to tell stories in different ways. Children can then be encouraged to exercise their own choices and judgement in a similar way.

An excellent story to use for this kind of thinking activity is Rumpelstiltskin. There are versions of this story in every culture in which spinning is, or was, an important activity. The stories collectively are sometimes called The Name of the Helper and there are common elements as well as differences running through them. Making comparisons – comparing and contrasting – is an important thinking skill that could therefore be developed through work on such stories.

Rumpelstiltskin is also known as:

- Titeliliture
- Purzinigele
- Batzibitzili
- Panzimanzi
- Whuppity Stoorie.

The endings of the story vary considerably. In some, fairly watered down versions, the helper stamps his foot and storms off. Other versions, less pleasant, involve him pulling his foot off after he stamps it and it gets stuck in the floor. Growing less pleasant still and hence more attractive, to some of the children at least, will be the ending where he literally rips himself in two! On the other hand, there are happy endings where, as a more compassionate figure, he flies out of the palace on a silver spoon (Tatar 2002, p.124).

It would be possible for you to tell an assortment of 'pick and mix' Rumpelstiltskins. The children can discuss and decide on a name from those above and their favoured ending. You then tell the story incorporating the name and ending for that day and the children have contributed actively to the creative process.

Comparing similar stories

The ability to make comparisons, to spot similarities and differences is an important thinking skill. Again, Rumpelstiltskin is useful for working in this area. An English version of Rumpelstiltskin is called Tom Tit Tot. In this version a woman is ashamed of her daughter's greed. She lies to the king and pretends that her daughter is skilled at spinning. The king decides to marry the apparently skilful spinner, but in the twelfth month of their marriage she has to prove her skill by spinning five skeins of wool a day. The Rumpelstiltskin figure is described as a 'little black thing' that twirls its tail and unless the girl can guess its name – she gets three guesses every day for a month – she will belong to it!

In yet another variant, called Bad Weather, a goblin agrees to help a king build a cathedral and the king must guess the goblin's name before the building is completed or give the goblin his heart – gory!

Telling a variety of these stories and letting the children decide on what is constant in the tales and what varies would be an interesting exercise. You might use mind maps (see p.41 for explanation) and draw up one for each story. Alternatively, decide with the children on the points of comparison. So you might look at:

- the parent figure
- the powerful figure that sets the task
- the helper
- the task
- the time given for the task
- the discovery of the name
- the outcome.

Going deeper, you might consider the character of the 'helper' in the different stories. Is he (it is a she in Whuppity Stoorie) completely evil or does he have good characteristics? What about the ending? Do the children think it fair? What about greed in the stories? Does that vary?

Creating a new story

Once they have worked on a variety of these stories in this way, the children could then, in groups, invent a unique version of The Name of the Helper story, thinking about all the categories above. Can they think of a task that is more meaningful for our society than spinning? What would an equivalent, common task be?

The generation of new ideas, the exploring of suggestions, the need to choose between alternatives that come when groups create stories together are all excellent ways of extending children's thinking skills and their ability to co-operate. This is true whether children are working on a completely unique story, or their own version of a well-known one as suggested above.

If you decide to create such a story with a group of children, they will inevitably need to make decisions, because there will always be more than one idea. It would not be right for you to impose your own creative taste on the story – it is supposed to be a collective effort.

One thinking skills exercise that can be used in the creation of a story is 3–5–7. In this exercise the children get into pairs and have to think of three things. The 'things' in this context may be the characters for the story or the events that take place or the problems the characters encounter. So, to take the example of Rumpelstiltskin, the children would need to think of three possible names for the helper.

Then the pair finds another pair and they need to come up with five names. Clearly, negotiation and compromise are going to have to be involved here, together with each child explaining their ideas and listening to the others explain theirs. When I did this with Year 2, we stopped at this stage, as the level of negotiation required was already quite challenging. Older children should be able to then get into groups of six and come up with seven possible ideas for the story.

At this stage the whole group can exercise a final choice. The simplest (and fairest) voting method I've found is to give every child a brightly coloured star-shaped card (available from most stationers). I write their choices on other cards, which I put round the room on the floor. The children then put their star on the card of their choice.

The name they choose goes on the board (or computer screen) and you move on to the next category, for example, the powerful figure.

Exercising choice in this way empowers children – some children are given few opportunities to take charge in their lives – and it also teaches them one method for solving differences of opinion. Obviously, it is also an early introduction to citizenship and the practice of democracy. A further advantage to such a system is that it allows quieter children to have more of an active say in the final product.

You will discover, too, that letting the children make choices is not easy for teachers. When I do this with children I have to watch my own preferred characters being thrown into the waste bin and that is not easy for me either.

Another simple method for letting the children contribute to the creative process is to take just two of their suggestions and then ask those who want to choose suggestion 'a' to stand up and those who want to choose suggestion 'b' to stay sitting down. That is a quick way of getting a group decision on whether, for example, to have Little Red Riding Hood dressed in orange or purple today for a change.

These techniques can thus be used to make new versions of old stories – a time honoured custom in the oral tradition, or for a class to come up with a completely unique but collaborative story.

Storytelling suggestion

Tell one of these versions of Rumpelstiltskin. You might put the children's own names into the story or ask them for ideas for weird names to put in. Follow up the story with philosophical discussion. Later, tell a different version and use it to generate comparisons.

Rumpelstiltskin

A miller had one child – a beautiful daughter. And all day long he would boast of how talented she was, how clever she was, how kind she was. And at last his boasting reached the ears of the king, who summoned the miller to stand before him. Sadly, in front of the king, the miller's boasts grew even worse: 'My daughter can spin straw into gold,' he said.

Now the king liked gold – most kings do. So he summoned the miller's daughter and led her to a room filled with straw. 'Spin this straw into gold before morning', he said, 'or else you die.' Then he left her with the straw and only a spinning wheel for company.

The girl cried. She had no idea how to spin straw into gold. Suddenly, a little man appeared. 'Good evening, Little Miss Miller's Daughter,' he said. 'Why are you crying?' The girl told the little man how her father had boasted to the king. She told the little man that now she had to spin the straw into gold before morning or else she would die. She told the little man that she had no idea how to spin straw into gold.

'I know how to spin straw into gold,' said the little man. 'What will you give me if I help you?' The girl said she would give him her necklace, and the little man sat down at the spinning wheel and began to spin. 'Whrrrrrrr, whrrrrrrrr' went the spinning wheel (use an instrument here). And soon all the straw had been spun into gold and the little man disappeared.

In the morning the king was delighted with all that gold but the sight of it only made him greedier still. He led the girl to a bigger room, filled to the ceiling with straw and he said, 'Spin this straw into gold before morning ... or else you die.' Then he left her with the straw and only a spinning wheel for company.

The girl cried. She still had no idea how to spin straw into gold. Suddenly, the little man appeared. 'What will you give me if I help you spin THIS straw into gold?' he asked. The girl said she would give him her ring and the little man sat down at the spinning wheel and began to spin. 'Whrrrrrrr, whrrrrrrrr' went the spinning wheel. And soon all the straw had been spun into gold and the little man disappeared.

In the morning the king was delighted with all that gold, but the sight of it only made him greedier still. He led the girl to the biggest room yet, filled to the ceiling with straw and he said, 'Spin this straw into gold before morning ... or else you die. If you succeed, you will become my wife.' Then he left her with the straw and only a spinning wheel for company.

This time the girl did not cry, but waited for the little man to appear. Sure enough, he soon arrived and asked her, 'What will you give me if I help you spin THIS straw into gold?' The girl sadly told the little man that she had nothing left to give, so the man said, 'Very well, promise me your first-born child when you are queen.' The girl thought she might never become queen or, if she did, she might not have a child and as she had little choice anyway, she agreed. The little man sat down at the spinning wheel and began to spin. 'Whrrrrrrr, whrrrrrrrr' went the spinning wheel. And soon all the straw had been spun into gold and the little man disappeared.

The king was overjoyed and married the miller's daughter, as he had promised, for she had made him very rich.

Spring passed, and summer, autumn and winter, and the following spring, a son was born to the king and queen. The queen had forgotten her promise to the little man, but when the child was just a few days old, he appeared and asked her to give him the baby. The queen was horrified and offered him all her wealth if he would let her keep the baby. But the little man shook his head and said, 'No, a human child will be dearer to me than all the wealth in your kingdom.' At that the queen wept and pleaded so bitterly that the little man felt pity for her and agreed to give her a chance. If, he said, she could guess his name in three days, she could keep the child.

The queen summoned messengers and told them to bring her all the boys names in the kingdom. When the little man arrived, the queen asked, 'Is your name …?'

But the little man shook his head and said, 'No, that is not my name.

'Is your name …?'

The little man shook his head. 'No, that is not my name.'

'Is your name …?'

The little man shook his head. 'No, that is not my name.'

On the second day, the queen summoned messengers and told them to bring her all the strangest names in the kingdom. When the little man arrived, the queen asked, 'Is your name …?'

The little man shook his head. 'No, that is not my name.'

'Is your name …?'

The little man shook his head. 'No, that is not my name.'

'Is your name …?'

The little man shook his head. 'No, that is not my name.'

On the third day, the queen was close to despair. But her final messenger came and said, 'I travelled to the other side of a mountain, to the edge of a forest, and there I saw a little man dancing round a fire and singing,

> Tomorrow I brew, today I bake,
> soon the child is mine to take
> The queen will never win this game,
> for Rumpelstiltskin is my name.'

The queen was overjoyed and when the little man appeared she asked, 'Is your name David?'

'No,' said the little man, 'that is not my name.'

'Is your name Kieran?'

'No,' said the little man, 'that is not my name.'

Then at last, with a smile, the queen asked, 'Is your name Rumpelstiltskin?'

The little man was furious and stamped his foot so hard that it went through the wooden floor. When he tried to pull it out, he pulled so hard that his foot came off, and then he stamped again, even harder, and disappeared into the hole.

He has not been seen again from that day to this.

Tom Tit Tot (from East Anglia)

A woman baked five pies and told her daughter to put them on the window sill to cool. The pies smelt so good and the girl felt so hungry that she ate one. That was delicious so she ate another. After that she still felt a little hungry so she ate a third. The fourth smelled so good that she ate that too. Then she thought, 'I've eaten all the others, I may as well finish them off,' so she ate the fifth and final pie.

In the evening, the mother sent the girl to fetch one of the pies but, of course, she couldn't because she had eaten them, every one. When the girl told her mother what she had done, the mother was so angry that she spun the girl round and round, singing in a loud, angry voice,

> My daughter ate five pies today,
> my daughter ate five pies today.

The king was passing by and heard the noise. 'What are you singing about?' he asked.

The mother was ashamed of her daughter's greed so she told a lie. She said, 'I have a very clever girl here. I was singing,

My daughter spun five skeins today,
my daughter spun five skeins today.

The king was most impressed. 'I will marry your clever daughter,' he said. 'And for eleven months she will have good food to eat, and beautiful dresses to wear and do no work at all. But in the twelfth month she will have to spin five skeins a day or else I'll chop her head off.'

The woman thought what a good marriage it was for her daughter and she agreed. The king, she thought, would forget all about the five skeins, she was sure of it.

And that's what the daughter thought too, but he didn't. For eleven months the girl had good food to eat and beautiful dresses to wear, and she did no work at all. But on the first day of the twelfth month, the king shut her in a room with a little food, a lot of wool and one spinning wheel. 'Spin me five skeins by nightfall,' he said, 'or it's off with your head!'

The girl sat down on a stool and began to cry. Not only did she not know how to spin quickly – she didn't know how to spin at all! Suddenly, there was a tapping on the window. She opened it and there sat a little black thing with a little black tail. 'Why are you crying?' asked the thing.

'What's it to you?' said the girl.

'Never you mind,' said the thing, 'but tell me anyway.' So the girl told him about the king, and the wool and the spinning and the 'off with your head'.

'I can spin,' said the thing, twirling its little black tail, 'I'll spin the wool for you.'

'But what will I pay you?' asked the girl.

That* looked at her out of the corner of its eye and said, 'No payment. Just guess my name. I'll give you three guesses every night for a month.'

'And if I can't guess your name?' asked the girl.

'Why then,' said the little black thing, 'you shall be mine!' and that twirled its little black tail even faster and grinned.

---

*   The unusual grammatical use of 'that' instead of 'it' comes from the East Anglian dialect in which the original story was first told.

The girl thought she would be bound to guess the name in a month. 'All right,' she said, 'I agree.'

'All right,' said the thing and twirled its little black tail so fast you could hardly see it, then it took the wool and disappeared. That night it came back and sat on the window sill with five skeins of spun wool.

'Three guesses,' that said, grinning and twirling its little black tail.

'Is it …?' she asked. That shook its head and twirled its little black tail even faster.

'Is it …?' she asked. That shook its head and twirled its little black tail even faster.

'Is it …?' she asked. That shook its head and twirled its little black tail so fast you could hardly see it and disappeared.

The king was pleased with all the wool the girl spun, but the next day he shut her in the room again, with a little food, a lot of wool and one spinning wheel. 'Spin me five skeins by nightfall,' he said, 'or it's off with your head!'

As soon as the king had gone, there was a tapping on the window and there was the little black thing, twirling its little black tail. It took the wool and went away and came back in the evening with five spun skeins of wool.

'Three guesses', that said, grinning and twirling its little black tail.

'Is it …?' she asked. That shook its head and twirled its little black tail even faster.

'Is it …?' she asked. That shook its head and twirled its little black tail even faster.

'Is it …?' she asked. That shook its head and twirled its little black tail so fast you could hardly see it and disappeared.

And day after day the same thing happened. Every day the king shut the girl in the room with a little food, a lot of wool and a spinning wheel. Every day the little black thing took the wool and brought it back, beautifully spun, at night. The girl tried and tried, but she couldn't guess its name. And as the days passed, the little black thing grinned wider and wider and spun its little black tail faster and faster and faster. On the last day but one it grinned from ear to ear and looked more wicked than ever. 'Tomorrow,' that said, 'you will be mine!' and that twirled its tail like mad and disappeared.

When the king arrived he was pleased to see the skeins. 'It doesn't look as if I shall have to chop your head off after all,' he said and invited the girl to eat supper with him. As they were eating, he laughed and said, 'Do you know what happened today? I was riding in the forest and I came upon a clearing. There was a funny little black thing sitting at a spinning wheel spinning so fast you could hardly see. And it was singing to itself,

> Nimmy nimmy not,
> I'm Tom Tit Tot.

The girl gave a deep sigh of relief and smiled.

The next night, when the little black thing came and said, 'Three guesses,' that twirled its little black tail and grinned from ear to ear, more wickedly than ever.

'Is it ...?' she asked. That shook its head and twirled its little black tail even faster and reached out its little black hand towards her.

'Is it ...?' she asked. That shook its head and twirled its little black tail even faster and reached out its little black hand a bit closer.

Then the girl laughed and sang,

> Nimmy nimmy not,
> you're Tom Tit Tot.

The little black thing screamed in rage and disappeared. And the girl hasn't seen it, from that day to this.

7.

Stories and the Environment

In times past, people told stories to help them to make sense of the environment and the seasons of the year. Humans were at the mercy of the elements – a harsh winter or a wet summer could mean suffering and death. Creation myths attempted to make sense of the harsh realities of life in story form while other stories grew up around the creatures that lurked in wind, rain, fog and thunder.

Today in the west we are more or less insulated from the effects of the climate and the world around us. Sometimes of course, we are less insulated than we believe and a flood or storm surprises us and we feel once more the power and danger of nature.

It is important for children, indeed for all of us, to remain in touch with the world around us. Little as we may recognise it at times, we are seasonal creatures, influenced by nature and the environment. Losing touch with the seasons, forgetting the importance of the rhythm of light and dark, work and rest, may be part of what makes modern life so stressful.

Children, especially, need to feel in touch with their surroundings in order to flourish, and the environment is an important element in their well-being and in their education. The environment can inspire stories, provide a place in which to tell stories and become a story itself. Stories can help children look at the environment with wonder and respect and invite an imaginative response to the world around them. They can also help to mark the passing of the seasons and contribute to the sense of rhythm and security that is so essential to children's well-being.

Telling stories outside

Many European fairy tales are set in particular environments. Little Red Riding Hood and Hansel and Gretel take place in forests, the Three Billy Goats Gruff in a meadow by a mountain stream. Such stories involve movement – through a forest, over a bridge. Stories like these can be effectively told on the move. If you have a wood near by, all the better. Tell Little Red Riding Hood as you walk along and let the children experience the delicious thrill of worrying about what will jump out at them from behind a tree. Let them play at being the wolf, at scaring one another.

Even if you don't have a wood near by, the stories move from place to place and you can nominate part of your school grounds to be Little Red Riding Hood's house, Grandma's cottage, the place where the wolf first appears and tell the story as you move from place to place with the children.

A different kind of story to tell is the 'story' of the walk through the woods or the grounds of your school itself. What were the sights, what were the sounds, the scents and textures of the walk? You could do a 'sense story', collecting all the experiences of the walk together or you could go for separate walks and generate stories for each sense. So, go for a listening walk. Ban any talking at all. The children are just to focus on what they hear and remember it, so that they can tell you when they get back. Then, with the children, you make a 'sound story' of that walk: what did each one of them hear? How might you record such a story? In pictures? On a tape recorder? With words?

On another occasion, go for a looking walk and make a 'sight story' of that walk. How might you collect and record that story?

We do such activities with younger children but forget that older children and teenagers are also capable of benefiting from silent concentration on one sense at a time and from thinking creatively about how to use and reflect on what they have experienced.

Using the environment to tell stories

At different times of year, the environment has different things to offer the storyteller. Go for walks and see what you find and bring back. Perhaps each child might have a bag to keep what they find (remembering not to pick wild flowers in the summer – sketch them instead). When they get back, the children can use such collections in a variety of ways.

- Let the children look at their collections and see if they can think of a traditional tale to tell with their sticks and leaves and twigs.

- Look at the collections and ask the children to make up a completely original tale that is suggested by what they have found, including each item in the story.

- Pick a single item and tell its true story, researching if necessary to find out facts about it.

- Pick a single item and make up a fantasy story about it – a leaf might be a magic leaf, a twig might once have been the wand of a wizard.

- Ask the children to pick out their favourite item and then you, their teacher, weave a story that incorporates every single one. Let the children help as much as possible with their own ideas.

Stories about the environment

As in the last exercise, you can distinguish between factual stories and imaginative stories about the environment. The story of a tree's life cycle from acorn to oak tree is a tale of wonder in itself. Such factual stories can be told in different ways – orally, through pictures, through music and sounds. Some of the greatest composers wrote music that told such natural stories. The 'Blue Danube Waltz' by Johann Strauss is one obvious example. Collect such pieces of music and play them to the children.

There is another kind of story that you can tell about the environment that gives it personality and human characteristics. I am indebted to Lyn Barbour, a Scottish drama and dance therapist, for this idea of 'anima', stories about the natural world, in which children give a natural feature, such as the sun, the moon, a river, or the wind, a character, a life, and tell its story.

For example, the story of a river's journey to an ocean might start with the river as a young child, born in the mountains and growing stronger as it travels across the land; the story could include adventures, and creatures and people it meets on its journey, until finally, old and tired, it reaches the ocean and becomes part of that greater expanse of water.

Such stories have much in common with the nature myths and creation myths of earlier times and are an appropriate way of helping children respond to nature.

A simple way to start such work with children would be to take a feature like the wind and, on a windy day, ask:

- If the wind were an animal, what animal would it be?

- If the wind were a person, what clothes would they wear?

- If the wind had a home, what would the home look like?

The children can then take their favourite ideas and develop them further, and tell them to one another.

Another way of responding to the environment and the seasons through story is to put what is happening outside, at the moment you are telling the story, into the story itself. I was telling the story of The Selkie Wife on a windy day, when the seagulls were crying outside the window and the wind howled round the school. Rather than trying to ignore the noise of the wind and the gulls, I put them into the story I was telling, adding colour and vibrancy to my account.

On a hot summer day, put a comment about the heat into Hansel and Gretel or The Three Billy Goats Gruff. It gives your story power and immediacy to ground it in the world outside the window.

Light and dark are also features of our environment that children can respond to through stories. Our experience of darkness in the Western world is becoming more limited because of light pollution – we see the stars less well than our ancestors did. Children are frequently scared of darkness – as are adults. When there was a major power cut in recent years in America, people panicked as they experienced real darkness for the first time.

Greek mythology had Artemis as goddess of the moon and Apollo as god of the sun, her twin brother. Children might make up a similar story about light and dark, or the sun and moon, which could help them with fear of the dark, as well as provoking thought about an important natural phenomenon. Is the dark always frightening or might the dark be a kindly figure in such a story? The performance poet, James Carter, has a lovely poem called simply 'The Dark', which ends, 'why won't it come out till its night?/Perhaps the dark's afraid of light?' (Carter 2002, p.59). Children could take this idea and weave a story about the darkness as a timid character who hides from the light.

The stars themselves have always inspired stories. Research the constellations with children and find the stories that are associated with them. Make up your own collection of 'zodiac' stories, either based on the traditional animals and characters or on new ones that the children create for themselves in response to the shapes of the constellations.

Creation myths

Creation myths were the original anima stories, endowing the seasons and the weather with personality. Scottish creation myths and stories feature Beira, an old woman or hag who formed the mountains and lochs of Scotland and who rules each winter with her magic hammer. Lyn Barbour first told me the story of Beira and the version at the end of this chapter is based on an account by Donald Alexander Mackenzie, which can be found online (see Appendix 1).

I use my story box to tell this story and unroll a golden cloth over the top of an iron-grey one as spring begins to spread its warmth over the land. You might also create representations of Beira and Angus in the classroom, perhaps using the environment itself to make models or pictures out of leaves or wood or moss. When storms rage outside the classroom, the children won't need much encouragement to use their imaginations and relate the weather to the characters they have heard stories about and created.

Collect other creation myths to compare with the ones you know already. The Judeo-Christian creation myth is an obvious starting point and there is the parallel myth that C.S. Lewis created in *The Magician's Nephew* (1955) as Aslan sings Narnia into being.

The ancient Egyptians believed that a great mound arose from the vast expanse of primeval waters (similar to the Genesis account of the wind of God swooping over the waters). Different Egyptian cities had different versions of the myth. In one, the first god to materialise on the mound was called Atum, Lord of Heliopolis, who then sneezed and produced the twin gods Shu (air) and Tefnut (moisture). Thus the world's atmosphere was formed. Shu and Tefnut then had children, Geb (earth) and Nut (sky). Nut and Geb had four children, Osiris and Seth, gods of order and chaos, and their wives, Isis and Nephthys, and from these origins all other life came into being. I love the idea of a god sneezing creation into being and I am sure children will too. A large Egyptian-style frieze of the primordial sneeze would be well worth seeing!

A good source for such myths is *The Illustrated Anthology of World Myth and Storytelling* edited by C. Scott Littleton.

Linking stories to seasons and festivals

I found myself drawn to telling the Beira myth during a particularly cold February when winter seemed to be fighting back with a vengeance. Snow lay on the ground and the wind howled outside as I introduced children to Beira's wind hags and snow hags that savaged the countryside and made the people huddle in fear inside their houses. It is not a story I would tell in the summer – it would lack impact and effect. It is a story for early spring, to encourage us that warmer weather is on the way and that winter will be defeated once more.

Children need to feel the seasons of the year and to celebrate the changes they encounter in the natural world and in themselves. We used to have the festivals of the church to help us mark the passing of the seasons, but increasingly in our secular world these festivals are largely neglected and only Christmas and perhaps Easter remain to mark the changes of the year. This may be part of what adds to the stress and unhappiness of modern life – we lack a sense of connection to our communities, to the natural world and to anything larger than ourselves.

Schools can reintroduce community celebrations into children's lives and link them to the passing of the seasons, to the wider rhythms of nature and faith communities. Traditional stories and sacred stories can both be linked to certain times of year and to certain festivals to help provide continuity and rhythm in children's lives.

I help schools design a cycle of festivals that are meaningful and unique to their school. Each festival has a story or group of stories linked with it which the children hear at that time of year every year. The festivals are intended to enhance the life of the school, to enrich the curriculum, to build the moral, ethical and spiritual dimension of life and to provide opportunities for the whole school community to celebrate together.

One infant school I work with decided to have special festivals to mark the beginning of the school year and also the end. At the beginning of the new year they spent some time with a reflective story based on the year that had passed, looking back at the good things that had happened last year as a positive way of starting the new year. The first day ended with a reflective story of all that had happened that day, 'On our first day together we …'.

They marked harvest with a festival geared to charity and gratitude, with a North American Indian story about a village that forgot to say 'thank you' to the spirit of the corn. Advent was a special time for thinking about light in darkness and for introducing the Christian story of the birth of Jesus gradually through the month of December. The school linked the Christian story with explicit work on building happy memories and hopes for the future.

In the cold winter months of February and March the school observed National Storytelling Week and Performing Arts Week and heard stories about saints and about the monk Caedmon, who wrote the very first poem in the English language. This story involved the whole school in composing a song and learning a dance which they could do together at this and other festivals.

Easter, the celebration of new life and the coming of spring, was marked with a simple retelling of the Christian Easter story, focusing on the journey of Jesus to Jerusalem. The transition from darkness to light was marked with celebratory food and candles and lots of daffodils, and links were made to the virtues of kindness and love.

At the end of the school year, as thoughts turned to saying goodbye and also to holidays and the seaside, we marked the end of the year with the sea legend of The Selkie Wife and with thinking about the good times that we had enjoyed together over the year.

Each year, the same festivals and the same stories are celebrated so that the children experience the joy of familiar traditions and build up happy memories to look back on. The passing year is linked with and marked by stories that are felt to be appropriate both for the season and for this particular school community.

Storytelling suggestion

Tell children this story through autumn, winter and spring and relate the changing seasons to its characters. Children, like our ancestors, can exercise their imaginations and use them to respond to and understand the power of nature.

Beira, Queen of Winter

Beira was Queen of Winter and older than the land itself. Her skin was blue, her teeth rust red and she had one eye in the centre of her forehead. She had a magic hammer and when she struck it on the ground the earth grew cold and hard as iron.

Beira was Queen of Winter and people said that it was she who made the mountains and the lakes and the rivers. She carried a great basket on her back, filled with stones, and when they saw huge boulders lying in the fields and on the mountain sides, people said they had spilled from the basket of the big old woman.

For Beira was big as well as old. Her shawl was so big that she washed it in the sea as no lake was big enough to hold it and, in November, when the first snow covered the mountains, people said that Beira had laid her shawl on the mountain tops to dry to show that winter had begun.

Beira was Queen of Winter and she had servants – a wind hag and a thunder hag, an ice hag and a snow hag to serve her – and she watched the land from her mountain throne and waged war against summer and all growing things. She would call her hags to her and cry,

> Ride to north, south, east and west,
> Smite the world with frost and tempest.
> War I wage and forth I go,
> Let all plants die and nothing grow.

And that very night a great tempest roared across the land and every living creature cowered as winter covered the earth.

The hags rode on giant, shaggy goats and, in December, when the winter torrents poured down from the mountain sides, people said that Beira was milking her shaggy goats and streams of milk were pouring down over the high rocks.

Bride was Princess of Summer, with golden hair and eyes the colour of a summer's day. Beira was jealous of her beauty and stole her and shut her away in a castle. Bride was dressed in rags and made to work at impossible tasks, continually washing brown wool to try to turn it white. But wool doesn't turn white for washing.

In January, old Father Winter came to the princess and touched the wool and turned it white as snow and gave her snowdrops to dry her tears.

Beira was Queen of Winter and when she saw the snowdrops she raged in fury. She summoned her hags and cried,

> Ride to north, south, east and west,
> Smite the world with frost and tempest.
> War I wage and forth I go,
> Let all plants die and nothing grow.

And that very night a great tempest roared across the land and every living creature cowered.

Angus was King of Summer. He had golden hair, a golden cloak and a golden sword that pierced the clouds of winter like a beam of summer sunlight. He lived on the Summer Isle, a magical land that floats off the coast, and he guarded the Well of Youth whose magic waters would turn any one who drank it young again.

Now, in a dream, Angus saw the beautiful princess Bride and, in February, he left the Well of Youth, and the Summer Isle, to find her. And as his feet touched the land, the air and the earth grew warmer, and crocuses and daffodils bloomed.

But Beira was Queen of Winter and when she saw the daffodils and crocuses bloom and felt the warmth in the air, she raged with fury. She summoned her hags and cried,

> Ride to north, south, east and west,
> Smite the world with frost and tempest.

War I wage and forth I go,
Let all plants die and nothing grow.

And she struck the earth with her magic hammer and turned it cold
and hard as iron, and that very night a great tempest roared across the
land and every living creature cowered and Angus was driven back
towards the Summer Isle.

Back and forth fought Beira, Queen of Winter, and Angus, King
of Summer. Beira struck the earth with her magic hammer and turned
it cold as iron, and Angus pieced the thunder clouds with his golden
sword, like a beam of summer sunlight. But Beira, Queen of Winter,
was growing older and weaker, while Angus, King of Summer, grew
stronger and stronger. And, in March, on the first day of spring,
people said that Angus had found Bride, Princess of Summer, and
released her from Beira's castle and made her his wife.

And Beira saw her wind hag and her thunder hag, her ice hag and
her snow hag fleeing before Angus's golden sword and she wept for
her lost strength and her lost youth. And she fled. She fled across
rivers and through forests, over mountains and hills until she reached
the coast and looked down on the Isle of Summer.

And, while none were looking, and while Angus feasted with his
bride on the mainland, Beira crossed to the Summer Isle and drank
from the Well of Youth.

The years fell away from her and Beira grew young and beautiful
once more and she fell into a deep sleep until winter and her power,
should come once more.

8

Sacred Stories

Schools are required, in the UK, to pay attention to the 'spiritual develop-ment' of children. It is an area many teachers feel rather uncomfortable in tackling, but storytelling provides one practical approach to what can be an abstract and challenging subject.

Spiritual development has close links with religious education (RE), of course, but is not synonymous with it. Children do, hopefully, grow spiritually as a result of RE lessons but they may also grow spiritually as a result of many other aspects of school life: the quality of their relation-ships with adults, the respect with which they are treated, the existence of calm and beauty in their school environment, the passion and dedication of their teachers. Storytelling has an important role to play in both RE and spiritual development.

Storytelling and RE

All the great spiritual teachers have used stories to convey fundamental human truths and it is therefore important for teachers in schools to be aware of this tradition of telling sacred stories. Faith communities, too, use stories to pass on their beliefs, practices and culture to the next gener-ation. Sacred stories and myths are those that convey what is felt to be of the greatest importance about humanity and its relationship with the divine.

In his book *Spirituality and Education* Andrew Wright argues that religion is a controversial subject and should be treated as such (Wright 2000). Since religion still leads to war and violence, this seems a fair conclusion. Storytelling and open discussion of the issues raised by such stories, using an approach like philosophy or thinking skills, would seem a most appropriate way of responding to such a controversial subject. The teacher does not impose his or her own views but allows stories to speak to the children and provides space for the children to formulate their own questions and responses.

Stories teach through symbol and metaphor, and they work indirectly. This allows the listener to choose whether or not to engage with the ideas that they present. There is space for thought and decision making, which means that listeners can deliberate and weigh up what the story is trying to teach them. Telling children the stories of different faith traditions allows children to think for themselves and to decide what they make of the perspectives offered and the truths that the stories present.

Stories have another advantage as a teaching vehicle in a subject like RE. Stories show what believers think and feel about God. Though the events in a story may have happened long ago, the story is told in the present and engages the present experiences and emotions of the listener. In a sense, the listener is drawn into the events of the story, given a taste of what it felt like to be present, of what it feels like to be part of this story or this tradition. Through the story, listeners can experience just a little of what believers think and feel about God or the divine. The listener is not just engaging rationally through hearing the facts of the story, but emotionally and experientially too, having a small taste of the tradition that the story comes from.

Godly Play

Godly Play is a story-based method of spiritual development and religious education based on the Montessori educational tradition and also on the Ignatian spiritual tradition of imaginative prayer. Developed and brought to the UK by Jerome Berryman, an Episcopal priest and Montessori teacher, it is now used in churches and synagogues in the UK and the US and is also finding a wider audience in schools, prisons, old people's homes and youth centres – because stories are not just for children.

My own storytelling has been influenced by Berryman's work. In a Godly Play session, a sacred story is told simply to a group of children sitting in a circle. Each story has its own set of wooden figures and props and a cloth to tell it on. The story is told quietly, with lots of silence and no eye contact between storyteller and listeners.

When the story ends, Berryman recommends following it with what he calls 'wondering questions' (Berryman 1991, p.34), such as 'I wonder what part of the story you liked the most?' or 'I wonder what you thought was the most important part of the story?' When I have worked with children, I have found they respond very readily to the question, 'If you could be anything or anyone in this story, who or what would you be?'

The time of 'wondering' is for the children to explore their own responses to the story, not for the teacher or storyteller to give their own ideas. After time has been spent talking and thinking about the story, the children choose how to take their ideas further. They might retell the story themselves using the figures and other materials; they might make a model as a response to the story; they may paint or draw or write or use a sand tray to explore their ideas. This work is decided upon by the children and takes place, for the most part, in silence. How they respond to the story is left up to them.

After a period spent in this way, which can vary depending on the age of the children, the session closes with a return to the circle for a time of prayer and a feast. The feast is a simple but important aspect of the session. The food can be as simple as a biscuit or a piece of fruit and some water in a cup to drink, but it is served with dignity and grace. Everybody is served before the feast begins and each person has a serviette as a kind of table in front of them. When everyone has some food and a drink, a thanksgiving prayer is said and then everybody eats together.

Eating food together and telling the stories of faith together is something that all religious communities do, and this practice, within Godly Play, brings the two together in a beautiful way. Further information on adapting Godly Play for use in schools can be found in Appendix 2.

Other ways of telling sacred stories

Godly Play is one way of telling sacred stories in a classroom context, but there are of course others. I told this story about Guru Nanak to a group of children with profound and multiple learning difficulties.

The Story of Guru Nanak

Long, long ago there was a man called Nanak.

Nanak loved God. Every morning he got up early and went to the river to wash.

Nanak listened to the sound of the water.

Nanak went under the water to wash.

Nanak came out of the water and sang songs about God and about God's love.

And then Nanak went home.

One day, Nanak got up early and went down to the river to wash.

Nanak listened to the sound of the water.

Nanak went under the water to wash.

But Nanak did not come out.

His friends were sad.

They looked for Nanak.

But they could not find him.

They were very, very sad.

They sat by the river and waited. They waited one day. They waited two days. On the third day, Nanak came out of the water and sang songs about God and about God's love. Nanak had seen God. God told Nanak to sing his songs to everyone.

Nanak's friends were very happy. They listened to Nanak's songs about God and about God's love.

This version of Guru Nanak was first published in *RE Today* (Fox Eades 2004).

The children had very little receptive language, so I kept the story simple and rhythmical so that they could enjoy the sound, if not the meaning, of the language. I created a sacred space in the classroom using a gazebo, some fairy lights and beautiful cloths, and we took the children into and out of the space as the story talked about Guru Nanak going down to the river and coming back again. I linked the name, Nanak, with a bell that I rang each time I said it. We poured water for the children to hear and touch when water was mentioned in the story. The river was represented by a long flowing cloth inside the gazebo for the children to touch and go under when Nanak went under the water. When Nanak came out and sang songs about God's love, I played a beautiful tape of choral religious music.

I told the story several times so that the children could experience repetition of words and sounds. Following up the story with questions or thinking time would not have been appropriate because of the children's language level, so the children's teacher and I kept the silence and stillness by massaging the children's hands with scented oils.

Though these children could not articulate their responses, their enjoyment of and engagement in the story was very clear.

These children had complex learning difficulties. However, this kind of multi-sensory storytelling and the creation of a sacred space in which to tell stories would be effective for any children.

Putting children into sacred stories

It is also possible to tell sacred stories and to have the children themselves become part of the storytelling. This is a particularly useful technique if you are telling stories to larger groups of children, such as in an assembly. Telling stories in an assembly is more challenging than in the classroom. I heard of one professional storyteller who refuses to work with groups of over thirty and who won't work in a school hall!

It is certainly more difficult to build a rapport with a larger group, but it is possible, and letting the children have things to see and do helps a great deal. I adapted one of Berryman's stories for Advent to use in a series of infant school assemblies throughout December. While the children watched, I began to build a road out of pebbles that led towards Bethlehem, represented by an empty crib in front of a screen. I told the children we would meet different characters on the road, starting with Isaiah, one of the Old Testament prophets whose prophesies are seen as pointing the way to Jesus. One of the children stood up and walked a little way along the road, being Isaiah for us, and I spoke the famous words of Isaiah, 'The people who walked in darkness have seen a great light.' The child who was Isaiah then lit a candle for Isaiah in an Advent wreath.

In the next assembly, I made the road a little longer, setting it out while the children watched, creating a silence and stillness in the hall in which to tell the story. Another child stood up and walked along the road as Isaiah and two more joined him, as Joseph and Mary. I spoke Isaiah's words again and then added the words of the angel to Mary, 'Do not be afraid ... you will give birth to a son and you will name him Jesus.' The children then lit Isaiah's candle and Mary's candle on the Advent wreath.

In three subsequent assemblies the same process was repeated. Isaiah, Joseph and Mary, represented by different children each day, were joined by some shepherds and some kings and one more candle was lit each time. On the final assembly, just before Christmas, the last candle was lit for the Christ child and every child in the school walked along the now complete road to Bethlehem and laid a star, with a Christmas wish written on the back, by the manger.

This was a simple use of storytelling to build in the children a sense of the wonder and hope that Christmas can contain. The teachers in this particular school also commented on the calmness that this approach produced in what is usually a frenetic term. Several said that it felt like a much more spiritual Christmas than usual.

Stories of hope

There are qualities that are common to all religious traditions that can be conveyed well through storytelling. Qualities like hope and thankfulness, courage and faith, forgiveness and kindness. Telling stories that show these qualities at work in ordinary people's lives is an important part of helping children to grow spiritually. They need not be famous or traditional stories, just simple stories that have inspired you and may similarly inspire the children you teach.

Scour the newspapers. Mostly they report bad news, but just occasionally a newspaper slips up and something truly inspiring creeps in! Such stories need to be seized and used to counter the prevailing idea that life is awful everywhere. It isn't – life is also full of wonder and goodness and courage, but these things are rarely seen as newsworthy.

One example is a story that older children might appreciate. It is based on a newspaper article I read recently and might appropriately be called

Never Again

There was a town in what is now the Czech Republic, a town called Kojetin. For five hundred years, Jews and Christians had lived alongside each other in Kojetin, more or less in peace. On the Sabbath day, the Jews gathered in their synagogue to hear the stories of their forefathers read from five books or scrolls which were called the Five Books of Moses, and to offer prayers to God in their own particular way.

But then there came a group of people who thought they were better than the Jews. They were based in Germany and they were called Nazis. They invaded the Czech Republic and, one morning, the people of Kojetin woke to see their Jewish friends and neighbours being led away by soldiers. Old people and young people, men, women and children were taken away, and none ever returned. They were killed, like many other Jews, because the Nazis had decided that one group of people was better than another.

For years, the Five Books of Moses lay in a warehouse, silent. Then, after the war, when the Nazis had been defeated, the scrolls of Kojetin were found new homes. Some went to America, but one came to England, to a new synagogue in Maidenhead where, once more, Jewish voices read the stories of their forefathers from the Books of Moses and prayers were offered to God, by these English Jews, in their own particular way.

Then one day in 1992, fifty years after the Jews of Kojetin had been taken away because the Nazis had decided that one group of people was better than another, a group of English Jews from Maidenhead decided to visit Kojetin. They found that the synagogue was now a church and that prayers were still said there. They found that the leader of that church had been praying for the lost Jews of Kojetin every year. They found that they were welcome in Kojetin.

And a service was held and the stories of the Jews were read once more from the Books of Moses as they had been read so long ago and prayers were offered to God in the Jews' own particular way, and the people of the town joined them and told of their sadness at seeing their Jewish friends led away. The people of Kojetin and their visitors offered a prayer together, let it never happen again.

Saints' stories

Every religious tradition has its special people and they, too, are a wonderful source of stories to inspire and encourage. The stories may be those of well-known saints or holy people, or lesser known ones that seem important to you. Again, these are stories to encourage and inspire, stories about kindness and faith and wisdom. One of my favourite saints' stories is that of St Werburga, a Cheshire saint, who might be called the patron saint of vegetarians because she resurrected a goose! It is a story that shows the importance of little acts of kindness.

Storytelling suggestion

Tell the story of Werburga and ask the children to listen out for the sounds and actions that the geese make. A noisier version would be to let the children hiss and honk. A quieter way of telling this would be to ask the children to make the shape of a goose's head with their hand and to pretend, silently, to 'hiss and honk and shake their great long snake-like necks' at the appropriate parts of the story.

One of My Geese is Missing

Werburga was a saint, everybody said so, and they told stories about her kindness. But Werburga said she just looked and listened and noticed the important things in life. She noticed the old woman who washed her clothes in the stream that ran past her cornfield and smiled when she saw her. And when, one day, the woman seemed more tired than usual, Werburga noticed and helped her to carry the heavy washing back to the town. Werburga thought old ladies were important and ought to be noticed.

Werburga was a saint, everybody said so, and they told stories about her kindness. But Werburga said she just looked and listened and noticed the important things in life. She noticed the children who played in the fields next to her cornfield and she smiled when she saw them. And when, one day, a little boy lost his favourite wooden horse in a clump of grass, Werburga noticed and helped him to look for it and stayed with him until it was found and his tears had dried and he was smiling again. Werburga thought children were important and ought to be noticed.

Werburga was a saint, everybody said so, and they told stories about her kindness. But Werburga said she just looked and listened and noticed the important things in life. She noticed the animals and birds who lived in and around her cornfield and she smiled when she saw them. She watched them feeding and squabbling and when, one day, a sparrow hurt its wing and couldn't fly, Werburga noticed and picked it up and fed it until its wing was healed and it could fly away. Werburga thought sparrows were important and ought to be noticed.

Werburga was a saint, everybody said so, and they told stories about her kindness. But Werburga said she just looked and listened and noticed the important things in life. But when, one evening, she noticed a flock of geese trampling her corn with their great, webbed feet, as they settled down to sleep, she didn't smile at all. She frowned, and called a neighbour and told him to tell the geese they could sleep in her barn instead.

Werburga never said very much. Mostly she just looked and listened, but people said she was a saint, so when she did say something, they paid attention. And the neighbour did as she asked, though he thought the geese would ignore him and only hiss at him and honk at him and shake their great long snake-like necks at him. And when the neighbour told the geese to follow him to Werburga's barn, they did hiss at him and honk at him and shake their great long snake-like necks at him, but they followed him all the same.

The next morning, Werburga went to the barn and opened the door. She looked and listened as the geese waddled out of the barn hissing and honking and shaking their great long snake-like necks. Then Werburga noticed something. She noticed that the geese were hissing more sadly than usual. She noticed that their honks were not as loud and fierce as they usually were. She noticed that they were shaking their great long snake-like necks from side to side as if they were trying to tell her something. And then she noticed that one of the geese was missing.

She called her neighbour and asked him where the missing goose had gone. The neighbour hung his head in shame. He had thought no one would notice if he took one of the geese. He had thought no one would notice if he killed that goose and ate it for his supper. But the geese had noticed, and so had Werburga. Werburga looked and listened and noticed things.

Werburga told her neighbour to fetch the bones of the goose he had eaten. And then she prayed, hard, because Werburga thought geese were important and ought to be noticed, and God must have thought so too because, as she prayed, the bones of the goose started to move and fit together, and as she prayed some more, flesh began to cover the bones and, as she prayed some more, feathers began to sprout out of the flesh, and soon there was a live, hissing, honking goose waving its great long snake-like neck at her, where before there had only been a pile of bones.

And the goose lowered its great long snake-like neck and it bowed to Werburga, to thank her for her kindness in noticing that it was missing. And all the other geese did the same. And then they spread their wings and with a last great honk they launched themselves into the air and flew away.

So when you see geese flying overhead, and hear their honks filling the air, remember Werburga who looked and listened and noticed the important things in life.

9.

Storytelling across the Curriculum

There are two ways of approaching the cross-curricular use of stories. One is to start with each subject and then look at how stories and storytelling might add richness and depth to the children's learning. To an extent, some other chapters in this book already take this approach – there are discussions of stories and thinking skills, sacred stories (which are clearly relevant to religious education (RE), stories and the environment (which might help extend thinking about geography).

The other way of thinking about the use of stories across the curriculum is to start instead with the story itself and to think about how a single story, or family of stories, might enrich each subject in turn. This approach has much in common with what used to be thought of as topic-based teaching, a method that lost favour for a while (because teaching is subject to fashion as much as anything else), but which is now gaining currency once more. It is an important approach, because it enables children to make connections between different areas of their learning, and the ability to make such connections is a core aspect of intelligence. This chapter will address both these approaches.

Using stories in individual subject areas

It is quite simple to see the relevance and use of stories to some subjects. Teachers have always used stories to help, for example, with the teaching of RE and literacy. Other subjects have less obvious connections but can still benefit from the use of storytelling.

Stories and history

History is an area where storytelling has less prominence than it might do. History is really all about stories and a good historian is a good story-teller. One of my favourite history books of recent years is Elizabeth by David Starkey (2001). It is a gripping story, beautifully told. Starkey's storytelling skills make history come alive.

Historical stories are, of course, based in fact, but as any historian knows, there is also a great deal that is subjective about history – no two accounts of any incident are the same and personal opinions and beliefs always colour historical accounts.

Telling stories from more than one viewpoint is an important histori-cal skill. Take a subject like the Viking invasions. Much of our view of the Vikings is derived from the stories told by the Saxons whom they came to fight and from later, Christian, historians. These authorities were clearly not objective and, though they painted the Vikings as murderous pagan thugs, the Christian Saxons of the same period were by no means gentle or averse to committing the occasional massacre themselves.

Taking a single event and weaving two stories about it – one from the Saxon and one from the Viking viewpoint – would help children to understand, in quite a practical way, the importance of perspective.

The stories told by groups of people also tell you something about their outlook on life and their beliefs. The Norse sagas are a difficult group of stories to use with children, but they do contain wonderful nuggets that can be lifted out and used. There is one Norse saga that is set in Britain, for example. It is about the Viking rulers of Orkney and is called the Orkneyinga Saga. Written in Iceland in the twelfth century it is based, like all the sagas, on earlier oral tales. The names by themselves might inspire the children to make up stories – 'Olaf the White', 'Aud the Deep-Minded', 'Thorir Tree-Beard' (J.R.R. Tolkein borrowed a lot of names from Norse sagas, including Gandalf) and, most wonderful of all,

'Thorfinn Skull-Splitter'. It is a bloody tale, containing much treachery, most of it in dispute over land. One story that older children might like to work on is the tale of the death of Sigurd the Powerful.

The Death of Sigurd the Powerful

Sigurd was earl of Orkney. A meeting was arranged between him and a man called Maelbrigte, Earl of Scots, to settle their differences. Each of them agreed to bring forty men to the battle, but Sigurd broke his word and took eighty instead, mounted on forty horses so that Earl Maelbrigte wouldn't notice until it was too late.

The Scots realised that they had been tricked but swore that each of them would kill at least one man before he died. Sigurd had his extra men dismount and surround the Scots, and it wasn't long before Maelbrigte and all his men were dead. Sigurd had their heads cut off and strapped to the victors' saddles to show off his triumph and off they rode back home.

However, on the way, as Sigurd went to spur his horse, he struck his leg against a tooth sticking out of Maelbrigte's skull. The tooth broke Sigurd's skin and the wound became infected. Within days, the treacherous Earl was dead.

(Adapted from Pálsson 1981, p.27)

This story would lend itself to retelling, to dramatisation, to art work or to an exploration of Viking culture.

Another way of using stories to enrich history is to take legends and try to pick out fact from fiction and explore the events and culture that lay behind the legends. A good example would be the legend of Robin Hood. Set against a backdrop of the Norman invasion, Robin was a Saxon hero. Why did the Saxons need heroes? Were the Normans villains? How good a king was Richard the Lionheart? What do the children make of the crusades?

Scholars disagree over whether Robin Hood has any basis in fact. The story first surfaced in a medieval poem called Piers Plowman in the fourteenth century, but for hundreds of years children have loved it as a morality tale of good conquering evil, the underdog outwitting the powerful enemy.

According to some versions, Robin was an arrow maker who went on the run after he killed a Norman. In others, he is a Saxon nobleman. Find out what you can, with the children, about the cultural and geographical background – what was England like at the time Robin Hood is set? Who are the real historical figures in the story and who are probably invented?

Stories and science

The story of how an acorn grows into an oak tree, of how a volcano erupts, of how animals reproduce, are all amazing tales in their own right, and children can be encouraged to appreciate and tell these stories of natural history. There are also amazing and inspiring stories about the scientists who have increased our understanding of the world and these, too, are a good way of encouraging children in their own scientific explorations. I find Bill Bryson's book, *A Short History of Nearly Everything* (2003) a wonderful source of stories about science and scientists.

Take, for example, the story of the discovery of Pluto, the ninth planet (recently astronomers have discovered a possible tenth planet, called Phoebe, but are not yet agreed over whether it is actually a planet). The discovery of Pluto was largely due to an astronomer called Percival Lowell. He funded the building of a famous observatory (named after him) and also believed that Mars was covered with canals, built by Martians to carry water from their polar regions to the lands nearer the Martian equator. He was wrong about that but right about the existence of a ninth planet, out beyond Neptune. This more accurate belief was based on the irregularities that he discovered in the orbits of Uranus and Neptune, and he devoted the last years of his life to trying to discover it.

Exhausted by his work, he died in 1916, without having discovered the planet he was looking for. However, in 1929, to draw attention away from the now embarrassing ideas about Martian canals, the Lowell Observatory resumed the search for the ninth planet and it was at last discovered in 1930 by a young man called Clyde Tombaugh. Lowell had predicted a massive gassy giant of a planet – like Jupiter. He was wrong, but was credited with its discovery, while Tombaugh, who actually found it, has been largely forgotten. As for Pluto itself, no one is really sure what it is like. We don't know what it is made of, what its atmosphere is like, even how big it really is. And there are still astronomers who don't really think Pluto's a planet at all!

Or there is the story of James Hutton, the eighteenth-century scientist who is seen as the founder of the science of geology and who transformed our understanding of the earth.

Hutton was a wealthy gentleman farmer who had studied everything from medicine to minerals. Looking at his farmland he realised that soil was formed by the erosion of rocks and that it was continually being washed away by rain and rivers and deposited elsewhere. Since this process was continuous, Hutton realised that some other process must be lifting up the land to create new hills and mountains to keep the cycle going, otherwise the earth would end up quite flat. He decided that this other process must be the result of heat within the earth. Marine fossils on mountain tops, he saw, were not deposited during floods, as some people then thought, but when the mountain tops were at the bottom of the sea.

His ideas were so advanced for his time that they were not fully understood for two hundred years. Unfortunately, Hutton, though a brilliant scientist, was an incredibly bad writer. His work was almost unreadable – long, complicated, badly written and much of it in French. It was therefore only after his death that a friend, who was not only a good writer but also understood Hutton's ideas, produced a simplified version of Hutton's book and the science of geology could be said to have been properly started (Bryson 2003, p.92).

Children who are starting out as scientists need to be inspired and encouraged by stories of the first scientists – who made mistakes, like Lowell, and who were not good at everything, like Hutton, but who took forward our understanding of the world around us.

Stories and maths

Not being a mathematician, and sharing many of the common emotional misgivings about maths in general and my maths ability in particular, the idea of maths and stories was not a natural one to me. Then I was fortunate enough to meet and work with Barbara Carr, a very gifted teacher and consultant, who introduced me to the fun and playfulness of maths teaching at its best and who uses stories extensively in her work with children who find maths difficult. Barbara's details are given in Appendix 2.

The basic principle of good maths teaching is to be as creative as possible and to let the children do the same. Barbara gives the example of some children struggling to understand place value once they moved beyond hundreds, tens and units and on to five, six and seven figure numbers. Barbara drew the usual columns but on impulse added a roof to the first three columns and left a gap before the second three. They could be terraced houses, she decided, inhabited by characters from Coronation Street. The poorest character lived in the units house but the tens house was posher and the hundreds house posher still. For the next three columns, semis rather than terraced houses, the children decided Brookside would be a good name and so on as the numbers grew. Adding in ideas of people visiting one another (but no more than nine would fit in a house) and a zero sign to show there was no one in, and you can see how Barbara's 'Soap Opera' numbers would alleviate anxiety, promote understanding and allow children to relax and have fun with mathematics.

Both teacher and children can use their creative skills to the full in such a lesson, and if you have artists and dramatists in the class, so much the better. Create a maths-based story-play with the maths, illustrate it, act it out, write it out, make up a tune to go with it. The maths will be understood at a deeper level and, importantly, some of the fear that often goes with it will have been reduced.

You can also use traditional stories. Barbara uses the troll from The Billy Goats Gruff as the decimal point who roars as the goats (numbers) cross his bridge. Another use of this fairy tale would be for multiplication tables. The smallest billy goat takes tiny steps, his hooves hit every other plank on a bridge where each plank is numbered in sequence, so he lands on the second, then the fourth, then the sixth plank and so on as he taps out the two times table. The medium-sized goat would land on every third plank, or every fourth or every fifth and so his feet would tap out those tables. The biggest billy goat would be landing on more widely spaced planks, six or seven or eight or nine planks apart. Children could draw the bridge and fit in the footsteps on paper. You could ask what number the first goat hits at his third step or his sixth step and a roar from the troll would greet mistakes. Provided they don't make deliberate mistakes to get the troll to roar, this method makes mistakes bearable and interesting rather than scary, which is what, in all learning, they really need to be.

Get the children up from their desks, go outside and draw the bridge with chalk on the playground with each plank numbered. Nominate children to be the smallest goat, the medium-sized goat, the biggest goat. Let them decide which table they are going to trip trap out and play Trip Trap Tables. As they land, they draw a hoof print with the number inside it and then they can take it in turns to be the five times goat or the seven times goat and to leap from number to number. These children will be enjoying tables and learning them at the same time.

Start with a story

The other way of approaching the cross-curricular uses of stories is to start with the story itself and see how it might enrich different areas of the curriculum. You can do this with any story and some might lend themselves more to some subjects than to others. It is important to follow your enthusiasm and that of the pupils and not to force connections where they are not apparent to you or do not seem to make sense. As an example, I shall explore the fairy tale The Wolf and the Seven Little Kids. Clearly, different activities will suit older or younger children and some will spark enthusiasm and others will not. Follow the strengths of the children and their enthusiasms.

Speaking and listening skills

Telling the story and helping the children to listen carefully is the first step. Then they could practice their own speaking skills by joining in with parts of the story. A further step would be to tell the story in a circle, sentence by sentence, the speaker wears a scarf and passes it on when they have finished. Using a story box helps to provide a visual prompt with this activity so the children can see the story as they tell it.

Let the children choose their own props and retell the story in pairs or groups of three.

Let them perform the story to an audience – you or another adult or another small group of children. Make sure the feedback is only positive at this early stage.

Literacy

I am indebted to Maria Duranti, a talented classroom support assistant from Riddings Infant School in North Lincolnshire, for seeing the possible application of digital photography when used with a story box. While children are telling the story using a story box, pictures could be taken at different stages of the story, showing the props in their different positions on the cloth. These photos could then become effective visual prompts both for sequencing the story, as the children place them in the correct order to retell it once more, and also for writing the story out.

A point of vocabulary would be to take the fact that young goats are called kids and find other names for the young of different animals.

Explore other beginnings and endings for the story. There are always different versions of fairy tales. The children might write their own, each with a unique ending.

The story moves between narrative and direct speech. Once the children have explored telling the story, this difference should be more apparent to them. If not, explore it with them and then let them experiment with putting direct speech into their story and noticing the effect that this has. Can they write a story with no direct speech? Could they write it entirely in direct speech? What would be the difference?

Maths

Children do not always deduce how many kids are going to jump out of the wolf's tummy. Younger children will benefit from work on seven and six and one more and one less than in this context.

Older children can explore multiples of six and seven. How many limbs did the kids have between them? How many limbs did the wolf consume? How many eyes did he eat? Had he eaten all the kids, not six, how many more limbs or eyes would he have consumed?

Or look at estimates of weight. How much would they estimate a baby goat to weigh? What would be the total weight of goat in the wolf's belly? What about a stone? Can they estimate the weights of different stones and deduce what size of stone the mother might need to simulate a kid accurately?

Science

The obvious link here is to work on sinking and floating. The wolf was pulled down into the water by the weight of the stones. If the mother goat had used pieces of wood, what might have happened? Or metal? Or paper?

Also, look at conditions for survival of living things. The wolf was hungry and needed to eat to survive. Wolves are carnivores – what does this mean and what else might the wolf have eaten? What other orders of creature are there? What are we?

When the wolf woke up he was thirsty. What is thirst and why does it occur? What needs water to survive? What else is required for survival of living organisms?

History

The story is set at a time when bread was baked by local bakers and millers ground flour. Explore the history of food production and the move to mechanisation. Or look at the changes in our environment – Europe used to be covered in forests and wolves were common. What caused this to change? Can they find the first written version of this story and look at the period in which it was written down?

Spiritual / moral development

Discuss deception and lies. Was the wolf justified in lying if he had to do so to survive? Is it ever right to lie? Was the mother goat justified in killing the wolf? Is killing ever justified?

Or think about vegetarianism. Should the wolf have turned vegetarian? Should we? What religious faiths encourage vegetarianism?

Music

Set the story to music. Make up a song for the mother to sing and for the wolf to sing and for the goats to sing when they are scared and when they are triumphing over the wolf's death.

Art

Victorian illustrators of books of fairy tales often used to produce single sheets of illustration for a title page that showed all the crucial scenes from a story. The children could, individually or collaboratively, produce such a sheet, either A4 or much bigger if preferred. Maria Tatar's book has some lovely examples of fairy tale illustrations which might inspire children to produce their own (Tatar 2002).

Cross-cultural links

I found an African story which is very similar to The Wolf and the Seven Little Kids. The children might look at similarities and differences between the two tales and then think about why some of the differences exist. If the story were set in a very different country again, what would it look like? What might it look like if set somewhere very cold like Iceland? Or somewhere tropical such as parts of India?

This is by no means an exhaustive list of the possible activities with which to follow a fairy tale like The Wolf and the Seven Little Kids. You would not want to do all of them – the children would be sick of the story if you did, and that is not the idea. Stay with it while their enthusiasm lasts and while the work is creative and fresh and rewarding. You do not have to cover the entire curriculum. Just a few activities on whatever strikes you as most profitable is a good idea. An older group of children might do different subjects, making decisions on how to follow up the story and following independent study paths according to their own enthusiasms and strengths. Then they could report back to one another on the work they had done.

Storytelling suggestion

Tell the Wolf and the Seven Little Kids and the African version, Dear Child, on subsequent days and compare and contrast the two stories.

The Wolf and the Seven Little Kids

Once a mother goat lived in a forest with her seven little kids. One day, the mother goat had to go out into the forest to find food.

'Stay inside', she said, 'and keep the door locked, or the wolf may get in and eat you. He may try and trick you into opening the door, but you will know him by his gruff voice and black feet.' The kids promised not to open the door until they heard their mother's soft voice and saw her white feet, and so the mother goat went out.

She had not been gone very long when there was a knock on the door. 'It is me, my dears, your mother,' said a gruff voice, 'and I have something for each of you. Open the door and let me in.'

But the little kids heard the gruff voice and they knew it was the wolf.

'You are not our mother,' they cried. 'Our mother has a soft voice and you have a gruff voice. You are the wolf. Go away!'

So the wolf went to a shop and bought some honey, which he ate to try to make his voice soft. Then he went back to the house and knocked on the door. 'It is me, my dears, your mother,' said a soft voice, 'and I have something for each of you. Open the door and let me in.'

But the little kids saw a black paw through the window and they knew it was the wolf.

'You are not our mother,' they cried. 'Our mother has white paws and you have black paws. You are the wolf. Go away!'

So the wolf went to a baker and made the baker sprinkle flour on his paw. Then he went back to the house and knocked on the door. 'It is me, my dears, your mother,' said a soft voice, 'and I have something for each of you. Open the door and let me in.'

The kids heard the soft voice and they saw the white paw on the window sill and they thought it was their mother. They opened the door and in sprang the wolf.

The kids ran to hide, but the wolf soon found them and gobbled them whole. All except the youngest and smallest kid who hid behind the clock.

When the mother goat returned, the youngest kid came out and told her what had happened and they wept together. But when they went out into the meadow, they saw the wolf sleeping under a tree. When they went closer, they saw something moving in his tummy. The little kids were still alive.

The mother sent the youngest kid to fetch her sewing scissors and some thread. She cut open the wolf's belly and out sprang the six little kids. Then she gathered stones from the meadow and put them into the wolf's tummy and sewed it up. The wolf slept soundly and did not know what had happened.

When the wolf awoke, he was very thirsty. He staggered over to a stream, weighed down by the heavy stones, but when he bent down to drink the heavy stones made him topple into the water and he fell in with a great big splash.

The little kids jumped with joy when they saw that the wolf had drowned and the mother goat knew that her kids would be safe whenever she went into the forest.

Dear Child

Once, a woman lived with her only child in a hut, in the middle of the African bush. It was a dangerous land, filled with monsters who prowled around looking for people to eat.

One year, the rains did not come when they should have done and there was a terrible famine. The woman said to her child, 'I must travel to a distant country to find food for us to eat or we will starve. It is too far for you to walk. You must stay here.'

The child was afraid to stay in the hut all alone, because of the monsters. The woman said, 'The monsters cannot hurt you as long as you keep the door locked shut. They may try and trick you into opening the door. When I come home, I will sing you this song so that you know that it is me and not a monster.

> Hello my dear child
> I am your mother
> Come now and open the door.

Do not open the door unless you hear me sing this song.'

The child promised and they ate the last of the food and went to bed.

The next morning, the woman left very early to walk to the distant country to find food, leaving the child alone in the hut. The child locked the door after the woman and sat, very quietly, hoping that no monsters would realise there was anybody home.

Soon, a monster came prowling around, looking for someone to eat. It sniffed at the door of the hut, but the hut was so quiet it thought it was empty and it went away.

When the woman returned, late that night, she sang to the child,

> Hello my dear child
> I am your mother
> Come now and open the door.

The child heard the woman's voice and opened the door. They were thrilled to see each other and ate the food before they went to bed.

The next day, the woman left early once again to look for food in the distant country. The child locked the door and stayed quietly in the hut. However, unknown to them, a monster had been watching when the mother returned the night before. Now, it came up to the door of the hut and sang, in a deep, low voice,

> Hello my dear child
> I am your mother
> Come now and open the door.

The child, hearing the deep, low tones of the monster, knew that it was not the mother but a monster. The child was very frightened and, of course, did not unlock or open the door. That night, the real mother returned and sang,

> Hello my dear child
> I am your mother
> Come now and open the door.

The child heard the woman's voice and opened the door. They were thrilled to see each other and ate the food before they went to bed. The child told the mother about the monster that had tried to trick its way into the house.

The next day, the woman left early once again to look for food in the distant country. The child locked the door and stayed quietly in the hut. Soon, the monster returned. It came up to the door of the hut and this time it sang, in a shrill, high voice,

> Hello my dear child
> I am your mother
> Come now and open the door.

The child, hearing the shrill, high tones, knew that it was not the mother but a monster. The child was very frightened and, of course, did not unlock or open the door. That night, the real mother returned and sang,

> Hello my dear child
> I am your mother
> Come now and open the door.

The child heard the woman's voice and opened the door. They were thrilled to see each other and ate the food before they went to bed. The child told the mother about the monster that had tried to trick its way into the house.

The next day, the woman left early once again to look for food in the distant country. The child locked the door and stayed quietly in the hut. Soon, the monster returned. It came up to the door of the hut and this time it sang in a soft and lovely voice,

> Hello my dear child
> I am your mother
> Come now and open the door.

The child, hearing the soft, lovely tones, thought it was the woman and opened the door. The monster burst in and ate up the child before it ran off, into the African bush.

When the mother returned that night, she found the door open and the child gone, and she knew what must have happened. As soon as it was light, she took her spear and her shield, and she went looking for the monster, deep into the African bush. Underneath a tree, sleeping in the sun, she found the monster. The mother saw that the monster's belly was bulging. The mother saw that the monster's belly was moving! With her spear the mother killed the monster and cut open its belly. Her dear child jumped out, alive and well.

The mother and child went back to their hut where they lived happily together once more.

10

Stories and Emotional Literacy

In recent years, the terms 'emotional intelligence' (Goleman 1996) and 'emotional literacy' have become widely used and are increasingly seen as an important part of a well-rounded education. In a recent report for the Department for Education and Skills (DfES), Katherine Weare and Gay Gray highlighted the importance of emotional intelligence for academic success, though they recommended the use of yet other terms, 'social and emotional well-being' and 'social and emotional competence' (Gray and Weare 2003, p.5) to describe this area of development. Whatever it is called, this area of intelligence may be summarised as the capacity to recognise one's own emotions and those of others and to manage and respond to emotions appropriately.

Teachers may react with horror at the thought of another subject to teach and another area of children's behaviour for which to feel responsible. One young teacher on a training course on emotional literacy with which I was involved asked, with some anguish, when she could stop being a social worker and start teaching. Others express concern that children are being encouraged to 'emote' in school rather than to learn.

These are understandable reactions, but they are based on a misconception. Learning and feeling are not separate activities, they are completely intertwined. Learning is an emotional event. So is teaching. Emotions are not a hindrance in the classroom, they are a blessing and a necessity. A child whose emotions are fully engaged in the learning process is a child who learns effectively. Positive emotions, especially, actually make children learn more easily. A teacher whose emotions are present and available in their teaching is a creative and inspirational teacher.

Children do not need to be encouraged to bring emotions into the classroom – they bring them anyway. Sometimes, as I have said, feelings support learning. As we all know, sometimes they can get in the way. Teachers also bring their own emotions into the classroom and our emotional awareness can be an important tool for effective teaching.

One of our tasks as teachers is to find ways of building the kinds of emotion that enhance learning and to minimise the feelings that get in the way. We do not need to teach 'emotional literacy' as a separate subject in order to do this. We can help children to become aware of their own emotions and those of others by using the opportunities afforded by the existing curriculum and life of the school. In Chapter 3 I touched on the emotional power of stories. Stories provide a perfect vehicle for raising children's awareness of emotions, for teaching them a vocabulary with which to discuss emotions and, a crucial part of emotional intelligence, for helping them to understand and think about the emotions of others.

If we ignore difficult emotions, will they go away? Regrettably, no. In fact, the opposite may often be the case. Ignore an emotion and, rather like an attention-seeking child, its behaviour will become louder and more obstreperous until it cannot be ignored any longer, and it bursts out and gets in the way of the task at hand. A little attention and a little thought and the emotion can be diminished until it reaches a manageable and useful intensity. All emotions have their uses. Even those we think of as 'negative', like anger and hate, can, in the right circumstances, be put to good use. A little anger is an important ingredient in assertiveness or the fight against injustice; a little hate towards acts of cruelty or unkindness can fuel a willingness to stand up for what is right.

The value of emotions in the classroom

Storytelling is an excellent tool for extending the emotional range of a group of individuals and for introducing emotions into the classroom in a safe and educationally appropriate way. Good stories cover the entire range of human emotions and struggles. Death, love, hate, envy, sibling rivalry and family breakdown are all found in the traditional stories that have lasted for centuries and will last for centuries more.

Telling stories that contain, either explicitly or implicitly, the full range of human feelings serves to introduce those emotions into the classroom and makes them available for thought or discussion. These emotions are already in the classroom, of course. Every human group, at some time, contains the full gamut of feelings and failing to talk about them does not make them go away. Storytelling is a way of bringing such emotions into the open and allowing them to be noticed, acknowledged and perhaps discussed. The discussion of these emotions is best done indirectly in the first instance, so that you are talking about something Cinderella is feeling, or the emotions of 'the witch'. In this way, the children do not need to make themselves vulnerable by owning to these emotions, either to others or to themselves, unless they wish to.

It is not uncommon for uncomfortable emotions, such as anger or hate, to be more or less kept out of sight even from ourselves. Thinking and talking about stories, or even just listening to them, allows children and adults to admit that such feelings exist and that they affect what people do and say. They may also then feel better about having such emotions themselves.

We all come from families where some emotions are more acceptable than others. Some families are uncomfortable with the expression of anger, for example, or with sadness. Children who feel deeply uncomfortable with an emotion practise what psychologists call 'splitting off'. They metaphorically build a wall round the emotion and pretend it isn't there. Children with lots of such internal 'walls' are going to have less of themselves available to think with and create with. Telling stories in which the full range of human emotions is expressed, from the deepest love and passion through to hate and cruelty, brings those walled off emotions back into the arena and lets children begin to notice them in themselves if they wish to.

When children can think and talk about the full range of human emotion, they will be more able to use those emotions appropriately for their learning as well as for their relationships.

That is not to say that emotions like anger or hate should be given full reign. Far from it. The more an emotion can be noticed and thought about the less expression it should need to be given. Children can and should learn to control their emotions – feeling anything is permitted, while acting on certain emotions is not.

Building an emotional vocabulary

An important part of children's emotional education is learning a vocabulary with which to think and talk about feelings. I have taught enough teenagers to find the phrase 'you're doing my head in' graphic but frustrating. What do they mean? How can you help to solve the problem without a more precise description of what that problem actually is? Building up a vocabulary with which to talk about emotions, and becoming accustomed to doing so, is an important part of a mature approach to life.

Children often lack the words to talk about feelings, either their own or other people's. The child who can say, 'I feel really cross that you have taken my bricks – I hate you', is less likely to hit another child with the remaining bricks because of the frustration inside them. If you cannot admit even to yourself that you hate someone, cruel acts actually become more likely because you act without thinking. Recognising and naming emotions reduces their power and helps us to control them.

To help children move beyond the level of 'she is happy' and 'she is sad', I have a series of cards with 'feelings' words on them. Daniel Goleman's book *Emotional Intelligence* has a useful list of emotions that you can adapt (Goleman 1996, p.289). Besides a list of eight basic emotions, anger, sadness, fear, enjoyment, love, surprise, disgust and shame, he then adds the family members of each major category. So, under fear comes also anxiety, apprehension, nervousness, concern, wariness, edginess, dread, fright, terror and panic. You can adapt the vocabulary depending on the age of the children and gradually extend the children's range of expression.

I find it useful to keep the concept of 'families' of emotions when introducing this work to children. In the 'sad' family come feelings like 'gloomy' or 'lonely' or just 'low'. In the 'happy' family come 'joyful', 'proud' and 'delighted'.

This is a list that I use, based on Goleman (1996) but with additions that seem important, such as 'thankful' and 'brave':

- angry, furious, cross, annoyed, hating

- surprised, shocked, amazed

- guilty, embarrassed, regretful, ashamed

- disgusted, scornful, contemptuous

- loving, friendly, trusting, kind, devoted, adoring

- scared, anxious, nervous, afraid, worried, concerned, terrified, panicky

- happy, joyful, relieved, content, delighted, amused, proud, thrilled

- sad, gloomy, grieving, lonely, desperate, depressed

- hopeful, faithful, brave, forgiving, thankful.

Strictly speaking the last items on the list are virtues rather than emotions, but they are important concepts for children to be able to articulate and think about.

My cards are colour coded, with the 'chief' emotion on a large card and the related emotions on smaller cards of the same colour. The four emotions 'sad', 'happy', 'scared' and 'angry' also have faces on, illustrating the emotions.

Children might be introduced to the cards gradually so that the families are built up and extended as they move through school. In nursery, symbols might be used alongside the words. One advisor I heard about has pictures of cats that illustrate different emotions!

I use a traditional story from Orkney, The Selkie Wife, to raise children's awareness of emotions. This tells the tale of a selkie, a seal that has changed into a woman, and who is prevented from returning to the sea by a fisherman who has fallen in love with her and hidden her seal skin. After seven years she finds the skin and returns to the sea, leaving behind her grieving husband and children. (See p.141 for the full story.)

After telling this story, I put the cards on the floor, arranged with the 'chief' emotion in the middle and the other, related emotions around it. In groups, the children discuss what emotions the selkie woman might feel at the beginning of the story and then they use voting cards, three per group, to choose which emotions she might have felt. I give each group three cards because I want to help the children grasp the concept of mixed emotions. It is possible to feel more than one thing at the same time.

Most children choose 'happy', but even the first time they do this activity, one or two begin to think more deeply. One child from a Year 3 group chose 'nervous' and when I asked about this explained that the woman might feel a little bit scared without her seal skin, as well as pleased to be dancing on the sand in the moonlight. The concept of 'vulnerability' was being touched on by this child.

Another child chose the card with 'amused' written on it to describe a possible feeling while dancing on the sand. When I asked about this, he suggested that the seals might have looked funny, being unused to legs, and she might have been laughing while she danced. What had seemed to me at first sight to be an arbitrary and slightly strange choice of emotion, proved on closer inspection to show some thoughtful insights on the part of this particular child.

The opportunity to discuss their choices, to say why they have chosen some emotions and not others, extends the children's ability to think and talk about feelings and to consider the feelings of another.

Without talking about their own feelings at all, the children are given the vocabulary to articulate emotions, at least to themselves, if and when they choose to do so. As Robert Fisher says in his book *Stories for Thinking*, 'They become able to look at themselves through looking at and thinking about others' (Fisher 1996, p.5).

Introducing nursery and reception children to 'feelings' words

In the younger years you might focus more on the faces and expressions on the cards than on the words. Telling a story like Hansel and Gretel, I have used a 'freeze frame' technique with a story box, stopping the story at a certain point and asking the children to think about one character in particular. Because I am using props on a cloth to tell the story, the children can literally 'see' which part of the story I am referring to and which character. Then, using the four principal emotions cards, 'angry', 'happy', 'scared' and 'sad', I ask the children what face, for example, Gretel might have had when she was all alone in the forest. Most children would opt for sad, but some children make some surprising choices. One child chose the 'happy' card and, when I queried this, explained that

Gretel might feel happy at having got away from the horrid stepmother – a thoughtful insight from a four-year-old child.

I give the children small cardboard stars so that they can place them on the emotions card they want to choose. This means they don't have to admit to choosing an emotion if they don't want to and there is no worry about having to write, either. In this way, the activity allows for the expression of what might seem unacceptable emotions, as well as acceptable ones. Gradually, one or two more feelings cards can be introduced for the principal 'families'. The children then have more choices to consider.

Thinking of Gretel's feelings again, but this time what she was feeling when she shut the witch in the oven, lots of children choose 'happy', but one chose 'delighted' to describe the character's emotions – with immense relish, it seemed to me! Most children love to hear of a child triumphing over an adult, doing things they would not dare to do or even think about, though all children are capable of hate and the desire to harm. Others, more sensitive souls perhaps, choose sad or terrified, the fear of the witch still lingering, or some identification with her leading them to choose 'sad'.

To extend their thinking about different points of view, we then think about how the witch felt at exactly the same point in the story, i.e. when she was shut in the oven. We compare these emotions with those of Gretel. One boy puzzled me on one occasion by saying that the witch felt 'relieved'. When I encouraged him to expand on this, it transpired that the lad, a lateral thinker, had invented an entirely different ending for himself in which the fire was put out and the witch escaped – his 're-lieved' was entirely understandable once I realised that he had created his own, unique context!

The children can see, in a very concrete way, that the same event felt different to the different characters involved in it and can begin to consider more deeply the existence of points of view other than their own.

Mixed feelings and different viewpoints

Good stories involve the fundamental human issues – good and bad, living and dying, loving and losing, trust and betrayal. They also contain characters that feel a range of emotions that children can reflect on and explore. The value of such exploration, as has already been explained, is that it allows children to reflect on common feelings and experiences without feeling exposed or threatened. You are not discussing *their* feelings or experiences but those of a character in a story. They may make personal connections if they wish, but it is not necessary for them to do so.

Because there is always a variety of characters in a story, feeling different feelings at different times, stories provide a perfect opportunity to reflect on the fact that the same event may cause different emotions in different people. The Selkie Wife is a good example.

After telling this story, you can reflect with the children on the feelings of the characters at different points in the story. With one group of children we considered how the selkie woman felt at the beginning of the story when she was first dancing on the sand with the other selkies, unaware of the watching fisherman. Then we considered how she might have felt when the fisherman refused to return her seal skin.

These emotions can be recorded on a simple chart. After you have considered the feelings of the selkie wife, you could consider the feelings of the fisherman at the same points in the story, and then of the children. The children will see, in a very concrete way, that the characters had different emotions about identical events.

Selkie

Fisherman

Children

⟶

Beginning   Middle   End

Emotions, of course, are not simple. To begin with, children are likely to respond that the selkie woman felt 'happy' at the beginning of the story and 'sad' in the middle and 'happy' at the end. Emotions are rarely single, though. We constantly feel a mixture of emotions, sometimes even opposing emotions at one time. It is possible to feel a mixture of love and hate, for example, or of happiness and sadness. Such conflicting emotions can cause confusion and distress for children. Being able to explore and articulate their emotional responses can bring relief from this anxiety.

It is also possible to feel different degrees of an emotion. Sadness, for example, might range from feeling a little low to absolutely despairing. Combining the freeze frame technique with work on families of emotions allows children to begin to explore and express a more complex understanding of feelings and motives.

Using storytelling to convey understanding of a group's feelings

Groups, as well as individuals, have emotions. Teachers know this instinctively, just as they know that wind and weather affect children's ability to concentrate and learn. Sometimes the 'class' is cross and irritable, sometimes it is hard working, at others it is playful or giggly. It is not just that individuals within the group are bad tempered or happy today – it is the group itself.

As the teacher, you are sensing the emotions of the group you are with all day long – this is one reason why teaching is tiring. You are tuned into the feelings of a large number of children and you are thinking about those feelings and responding to them appropriately at the same time as you are performing your more explicit role of teaching. Telling stories can be a useful tool to help you process those powerful group emotions and at the same time help your children to feel understood and listened to.

The stories you select to tell, and the way that you tell them, can let the children know that you are thinking about them, that you have noticed their mood and are responsive to their feelings. Allow space in your planning for spontaneity and to allow your own instincts to guide you. Set aside time to tell 'a story' but do not specify which story you are going to tell, or if you do, be prepared to change. Perhaps you were planning a gentle rendition of Goldilocks and the Three Bears. However, it was a wet, bad-tempered, windy day with no outdoor play times and they feel like killing each other and you feel like killing them. If you attempt a gentle rendition of Goldilocks, with the mood that you are all in, it will not work! The listeners, remember, contribute as much to the telling of a story as the 'teller', so the story has to suit their mood as well as yours.

Either abandon Goldilocks and go for something gruesome – The Billy Goats Gruff is good for anger, or Hansel and Gretel – or tell Goldilocks in a way that emphasises her 'badness' and selfishness and put in a little fear, too. Make the bears rather more scary than usual. Perhaps they could be really angry about what has happened or just thoroughly bad tempered – like the children that day.

In this way you are saying to the children indirectly, 'I have noticed your bad mood, I understand and am not intimidated by it, sometimes we all feel like that, even me.' The understanding of a thoughtful adult is profoundly satisfying and supportive for all children. Their bad mood has generated anxiety in the children – will you cope or will their 'badness' make you fall apart? Will you hate them and reject them? These anxieties are not necessarily conscious but all children feel them.

By playfully incorporating their bad mood into your storytelling you reassure them deeply and relieve their anxieties. No, you don't hate them, you are saying in effect. Yes, of course you can cope with their bad temper. As a result, tomorrow may well be a much calmer day.

Storytelling suggestion

Tell Hansel and Gretel several times then ask the children questions such as:

- Which character might have felt e.g. angry (or sad, or relieved, etc.) and when?

- What emotions might Hansel have felt at *this* point of the story? (You might wish to introduce emotions cards before this or you will probably just get 'happy' and 'sad'.)

Hansel and Gretel

Once upon a time a poor woodcutter had a son called Hansel, a daughter called Gretel and a mean and horrid wife.

One night, when their food was almost gone, the mean and horrid wife told the woodcutter to take the children into the forest and leave them there.

Hansel heard them talking, so the next day, when the woodcutter took the children into the forest, Hansel dropped a trail of pebbles so that he and Gretel could find their way home. When their father left them alone in the forest, the children waited until the moon came up and shone on the trail of pebbles, and they followed the trail, through the trees, all the way back to their father's house.

Soon, the family's food was almost gone again and the mean and horrid wife told the woodcutter to take the children into the forest and leave them there.

Hansel heard them talking, so the next day, when the woodcutter took the children into the forest, he dropped a trail of breadcrumbs so that he and Gretel could find their way home. But the birds came and ate the breadcrumbs, and when their father left them alone in the forest, Hansel and Gretel were completely lost.

They walked and they walked, they got hungrier and hungrier. Then they saw a bird, a beautiful white bird, who led them, through the trees, deeper and deeper into the forest until they came to a house. It was not their father's house. And it was not an ordinary house, made of bricks or wood. It was a gingerbread house, with walls made of biscuits, a roof made of chocolate and windows of sweet golden sugar.

The children were so hungry they had started to eat the house when an old woman came to the door and invited them in. She gave them supper, and beds to sleep in, and she seemed very kind, but the next morning she shut Hansel in a cage in a dark cellar because she was a mean, horrid and very cruel witch who wanted to eat him.

Hansel had lots to eat so that he would grow fat and each day the witch would ask him to poke his finger out of the cage to see if he was fat enough to eat. Each day, Hansel found a thin twig and poked that out instead, and because the cellar was so dark, the witch didn't realise that he was tricking her.

But at last the witch grew tired of waiting. She told Gretel to light the fire under the oven. She told Gretel to open the oven door. She told Gretel to climb into the oven to see if it was hot enough to cook! Gretel said, 'How do I light the fire?' So the witch showed her. Gretel said, 'How do I open the oven door?' So the witch showed her. Gretel said, 'How do I climb in the oven to see if it is hot enough to cook?' So the witch showed her and as soon as the witch climbed into the oven Gretel slammed the door shut and the witch was trapped.

Gretel released Hansel from his cage, and he and Gretel searched the house and found bags full of treasure. The children took the treasure and ran away from the gingerbread house, leaving the witch in the oven to die. They ran and they ran, through the trees, until they reached a river where a kind white duck helped them across. Then they ran and they ran, through more and more trees, until they came to their father's house. The mean, horrid wife was dead, so Hansel and Gretel gave their father the treasure they had found and they all lived together in safety and plenty.

11.

Storytelling and Reflection

The ability to reflect is an essential part of the teaching process. Just as a parent's efforts to understand a baby support and enhance that child's development, so a teacher's ability to step back and think about the class, about individual and group dynamics, about what and how the children learn, is far and away the most important part of teaching. More important than plans, visual aids or interactive white boards is a teacher's capacity to wonder about what is going on and to respond accordingly.

Reflection is also an essential part of learning. Reflecting on our emotions and the emotions of others is the first step in developing emotional literacy, and reflection on what we have been studying is a key part in developing a mature understanding of any topic. Peter Fonagy, a clinical psychologist, describes the importance of reflection and an awareness of the mental states of others in developing resilience, the ability to withstand difficult life events. Sometimes parents have not been able to encourage such reflection and awareness in their children because of their own difficulties in these areas. Fonagy asks whether the educational system might 'take steps to compensate and systematically enhance awareness of "other minds"?' (Fonagy *et al.* 1994).

Regrettably, one of the disadvantages of the national curriculum in recent years is that time for teachers and pupils alike to stop and think has been in danger of being squeezed out of the school day. It is well worth making the effort to put it back in because our teaching will benefit if we do and so will the pupils' learning. There are simple storytelling techniques that you can use for yourself and with the children to put in a little 'reflection time' at the beginning and end of lessons or the school day. The positive effects of such reflective stories, not only on academic learning but also on social and emotional skills, should easily repay the effort required to do them.

There are also ways of working with traditional stories that encourage reflection at the same time as they fulfil curriculum objectives. This means that they simultaneously help children to learn academically and emotionally, contributing to their long-term well-being while they improve literacy or speaking and listening skills.

Developing a realistic view of life

Some children, like some adults, have an overwhelmingly pessimistic approach to life. Studies show that pessimists are more at risk of depression and give up more easily (Seligman 1990, p.5). One defining characteristic of pessimists is that they see bad events as pervasive, affecting everything and lasting for ever. This kind of thinking is not only unhelpful, it is also often inaccurate.

Stories provide one way of learning to look at the world as a whole, as a mixture of good and bad events and of seeing reality more accurately. Most events, even difficult ones, contain some positive aspects and learning to see these positives is an important skill.

Practising the skill of optimistic thinking (and it is a skill) through thinking about stories may prepare children for using it in real life. Stories become a training ground, a safe space in which to practise these important life skills.

One exercise I use with children to encourage more accurate thinking about people and events is called 'good bits/bad bits'.

Good bits/bad bits

The first stage, for younger children, is to listen to a story and then to think about one thing they liked in the story and one thing they didn't like. After a story and some thinking space, the children tell me the things they liked and I mind map (see p.41 for explanation) their ideas in a single colour. Then, when everyone who wishes to speak has done so, I ask what they didn't like in the story and add these ideas to the same mind map but in a different colour.

Here is an example of likes and dislikes offered by reception children following my version of Little Red Riding Hood.

The children liked:

- the basket of good things to eat
- Little Red Riding Hood
- the wolf jumping out of bed
- the wolf eating Grandma
- Little Red Riding Hood picking flowers
- the wolf climbing into the bed
- the bad wolf.

The children didn't like:

- the wolf eating Grandma
- the woodcutter chopping off the wolf's head
- Little Red Riding Hood talking to the wolf
- Little Red Riding Hood running away
- the bad wolf.

What is immediately apparent is that the same things crop up in both lists. Some children liked the big bad wolf – and some didn't! The children can be helped to see that, in their group, different people have different views and that this is all right. They can also see that in a single story they can like some parts and dislike other parts. It is not a 'good' story because they like some of it, or a 'bad' story because something scary happens. It is a mixture; like reality.

This exercise looks at the story from their point of view. It is what *they* like or dislike about the story. The next step is for them to try to think about the story from the point of view of one of the characters. To think, for example, about Little Red Riding Hood. If she were looking back on what happened, what would *she* have liked and what would she have disliked about the events. Here again is the 'awareness of other minds' that Fonagy was talking about.

After telling the story, ask the children to think of one character and to decide what, from the story, would have been a 'good bit', something the character enjoyed or felt good about and what would have been a 'bad bit' – something that made the character sad, or scared or angry?

This process encourages children to begin to see things from another's point of view, but in a way that is not at all threatening. When engaged in the heat of a dispute over who should be playing with this toy now, children are frequently asked to 'share', or to 'think of how Joe feels' but, fired up with their own emotions, they find this very hard indeed.

Working through stories in this way allows them to practice the art of 'considering other minds' in a neutral setting, when they are not personally involved. Hopefully, the practice of this skill will then make them more able to think of others in real situations in which they are involved.

Awareness of mixed emotions

This is another technique for showing children that people can feel very different things about the same event. I did the good bits/bad bits exercise with some Year 6 children following the story of The Selkie Wife. I asked the children to work in groups of three and to think about the story from the point of view of the selkie wife herself. If she were looking back on the events that the story relates, which would she say were 'good bits' and which were 'bad bits'? The children were given small pieces of paper in two colours – one colour for the good bits and another for the bad bits. They were asked to draw or write one 'bit' on each piece of paper.

The children were called back into a large group and I asked one group for their three good bits. I wrote them down on a mind map and then asked if anyone had exactly the same things. If they did, they brought the pieces of paper out and put them next to the mind map. Then I asked for any different 'good bits'. Again, if other children had the same ideas they brought out their papers and put them next to the map. This technique for gathering ideas is a very inclusive one – it means that even quiet, reticent children have their ideas put down on the map. It is also a useful technique for keeping kinaesthetic learners happy and engaged.

We repeated the process for the selkie wife's 'bad bits' and found, interestingly, that the same event could fall into both categories. One group felt that the wife's farewell to her children was a 'bad bit' and another group felt that it was a 'good bit'. I put it in both categories and drew the children's attention to it. They were beginning to discover for themselves, from their own ideas and discussion, how complex, even contradictory, motives and emotions could be.

The children then went back into their small groups to think about the fisherman, what were *his* good bits and bad bits? We repeated the process of gathering their ideas onto the mind map and then reflected on it. Some of the events that they had classified as 'good' for the selkie wife, were classified as 'bad' for the fisherman and the other way around. Again, the children were discovering for themselves that different people could feel completely opposite emotions about a single event.

It is interesting, too, to reflect on what children consider to have been 'good' and 'bad' events. Their views are often very different from the views adults would express after the same story. All the groups of children I have done this exercise with saw the finding of her skin as a 'good' event for the selkie wife. When I did this with a staff group, none of them even mentioned it!

Letting children reach their own conclusions about stories rather than imposing our own adult interpretations is a valuable and enlightening process. We may be continually surprised at what children really think when they are given the opportunity to freely express their opinions.

'Reflective stories'

Reflection, i.e. taking time to look back over a day or an activity, is an important part of the learning process. A thinking skills session always ends with time to discuss what was achieved and how it was achieved. Children are asked to consider the strategies they have used to achieve a goal so that the learning process becomes explicit and they realise that they can use these strategies in other settings.

This, too, is a kind of storytelling. It is the 'story' of what the children were doing during the lesson.

When we have finished working with a story, I ask children to reflect on what they have been doing and I produce a visual map of their ideas that becomes a permanent record of their work. For example, after a session on storytelling, a Year 2 group suggested that they had been:

- thinking
- choosing symbols
- listening
- speaking
- storytelling
- looking
- turn taking.

I then turned their ideas into a simple story. 'Today, class 3 had a story-teller called Jenny to work with them. She told them the story of The Three Little Pigs. They listened carefully and thought about the story. They looked closely at her while she was telling the story. Then they worked together, choosing their own props to tell the story. They had to listen to one another and make choices. Then they told the story for themselves and Jenny was VERY impressed at how well they remembered the story, at the words they chose, at the skilful way they took turns to be the storyteller and at how they listened to each other, too. It was a really good session.'

My feedback, in the form of a story, was hopefully memorable, useful and affirming. It clarified for them the skills they had used and put their own suggestions into story form.

A Year 6 group can clearly make much more sophisticated reflections on the processes involved in their learning and swiftly see the potential of using their skills in other areas. A group, again following a story session, produced a visual diagram or 'story' of the processes involved in their work which included:

- thinking from other perspectives
- imagining
- understanding
- making decisions
- making judgements

- listening to a story
- listening to each other
- talking
- thinking by drawing
- sharing ideas
- learning.

Seeing what they have been doing in this way affirms the children as they realise what sophisticated processes they have been engaged in and it also builds their confidence. The teacher can add to the list too, congratulating a child here, emphasising how much effort she had noticed there. A teacher might weave the visual map into an oral story or leave it just as it is, a visual record of the story of a hard-working lesson.

Reflection is a kind of story – it is the story we tell ourselves about what has happened in the past.

This kind of story, which is a summary of a session in story form, reinforces for the children the strategies they have used, allows you to affirm their work and is more memorable than a simple discussion or list. It is a 'reflective story'. The human brain is a story-making and story-remembering instrument. You could scribe and record a story like this, perhaps from a single session a day, and look back on your daily 'reflective stories' at the end of the week to further reinforce the children's learning.

WWW – What Went Well?

Reflection is an important part of social and emotional development. Looking back at events, considering what went well and what was enjoyable, helps children to gain confidence and feel more positive about themselves and about school. Psychologists have found that depressed people have good and bad thoughts in a ratio of 1:1. Non depressed people have twice as many positive thoughts as negative ones. This is relevant for teachers because happy, positive children learn more effectively than unhappy ones.

At the end of Chapter 1 is a storytelling suggestion, The Story of Today. This involves, at its simplest level, making a record of the day's events in story form. 'First thing this morning we came into class. Then we … then we ….' This has obvious value as an exercise in arranging sequential information. It is also fun to do – you can do it backwards as well. 'Last thing of all, we went home. Before that we …'.

You can then use this technique to invite children to find the 'good bits' of the day. Any day, no matter how awful, has some good things in it. Finding those good parts and dwelling on them, rather than on the negative parts, is the hallmark of a resilient and healthy personality. By encouraging children to find and recall 'good bits', you are teaching them a useful life skill as well as rounding off the day in a satisfying way.

The psychologist Martin Seligman has an exercise called The Three Blessings. People are asked to record three good things that happen each day and why they have happened. Early research findings indicate that it is a powerful tool for decreasing depression and building positive emotions (Seligman 2004b).

I have adapted this exercise for using with children and I call it WWW, which stands for 'What Went Well?' This tool can be used in different contexts. In Chapter 5, I suggested using it for children to comment on what they think went well in a storytelling exercise. This uses WWW to build up the skill of positive listening.

It can also be used very effectively at home time to summarise and focus attention on the positive aspects of that day. When I have used this, I have asked children to think of three things that have gone well – taking a silent minute to reflect. Then I get them to tell me the best one and I write it up on a mind map on the board, making sure each child is heard and their best bit of the day is included. Then I tell the 'Story of 6J – WWW' back to them. Children enjoy this kind of reflective story and find it an affirming and positive end to a day. It also teaches them the important skill of positive reflection and building happy memories.

The next stage in WWW is to add a fourth W – Why? Why did these good things happen? The *why* is important because it helps to identify to what extent we are directly involved in creating the good things that happen to us. It also helps to build an analytic attitude that finds meaning and sense in life.

This is not an easy thing for children to do (some adults find it challenging too) and they may need help at first to see the part that they play. It is worth persisting with. The stories children tell to themselves, about themselves, have an important effect on their present happiness and future achievements. Influencing these stories positively is a valuable thing for any teacher to do.

Recording reflective stories

These reflective stories can remain as oral stories. Alternatively you might decide to record or scribe them sometimes and keep them as a record of your class's collective journey together. Looking back over the stories a term or two later would allow the children to see how they have changed and grown and developed.

One teacher I worked with decided to do a monthly 'reflective story', recalling with the children the high points of each month and saving them, in story form, together with photos that were taken over the course of the same month. They would be able, occasionally, to get out the album of photos and stories and reflect together on 'the start of term', or look at 'what happened in October'. A good strategy on a bad day would be to get out the positive reflective stories and to remember together a happy event. Recalling happy events has been shown to have a powerful effect on present mood and is an important positive behaviour strategy.

Class stories are one form of reflective story, but children could also do personal ones. A little booklet of 'my best bits of this term', or 'WWW' would be an affirming final task for any age of child and a good thing to take home and share with parents. Children could record their own WWW stories for a day or a week – as a mind map, a series of pictures or in words and keep them in a file.

Children with behavioural difficulties or an unhappy child might benefit from sitting down with an adult and looking back over their WWW stories. Seeing that they can affect their own happiness can give children a greater sense of control and it is often the children who feel the least in control of their lives who can be the most troubled.

Positive reflective stories for teachers

Positive reflective stories are important for teachers, too. At a staff meeting, I asked a group of staff to recall the 'good bits' of their day. At first there was a resounding silence, as a tired group of teachers struggled to recall something positive that had happened in the previous six hours. The human brain is wired to notice bad things much more easily than good ones. At the end of a day or an event it will be what went wrong that is at the front of your consciousness not what went well. Psychologists call this the Zeigarnik effect after the scientist who first identified it (Seligman 2004a).

It requires effort to counter the Zeigarnik effect and positive reflective stories are one tool for doing so. At this particular meeting, it took a little while before someone recalled a child who had succeeded in an area he normally struggled with. Someone else had seen a child being patient – a child who usually found self-control difficult. Another person recalled the children initiating an activity. I recorded their recollections on paper and gradually we built up a picture of a school where excellent things were happening and the staff were able to feel affirmed and encouraged by their collective recollections. The positive recollections seemed infectious – once they started, each person's memory jogged other thoughts and a virtuous circle was created.

We thought about and acknowledged the low points too, but we didn't record them. They were there to be learnt from – and moved on from.

Stories and endings
School life is full of endings and goodbyes. Saying goodbye to a group of children is invariably a mixed event – there may be relief, there may even be regrets, there will undoubtedly be some sadness. Reflective stories and traditional stories may all be used to help us achieve 'good endings' to the term or the year.

If you have collected reflective stories throughout a year, spending time in the weeks before you finish looking back over the happy memories would be an excellent preparation for the end of term. Children could prepare their own books of WWW for the year, highlighting the best bits and talking about them together.

If photos formed part of your reflective stories, the children would enjoy noticing how they had grown and changed, as well as looking over what they had learned. They would then be able to take the positive events of the year with them when they moved on. Looking at your reflective stories would form a focus for thinking about the sadness of saying goodbye to that teacher, helped by the pleasure of shared happy memories.

Traditional stories can also form an appropriate way of thinking about saying goodbye. I tell The Selkie Wife at one school as part of the Endings Festival at the end of the school year – it articulates the sadness of goodbyes and the importance of happy memories. It seems also an appropriate final story for a book about storytelling.

Storytelling suggestions

For a week, do WWW with your class. Include yourself in the exercise. What effect does it have on the mood of the children and their attitude? How does it affect you?

Tell The Selkie Wife and ask the children to reflect on the 'good bits and bad bits' of the different characters.

The Selkie Wife

Once, a fisherman lived all alone in a cottage by the sea. He loved the sea. Every evening he would walk along the beach. He would look out to sea, and enjoy the peace of the evening and listen to the sound of the waves on the shore and his heart would fill with happiness.

But though the sea, and the peace and the sounds of the waves on the shore made him happy, there was one thing missing – he had no one to share his happiness with and he was lonely, living all by himself.

One day, as usual, he went for a walk along the beach. He looked out over the sea and enjoyed the peace of the evening and listened to the sound of the waves on the shore, and his heart was filled with happiness.

Then he heard voices. He walked a little further along the beach and he saw people dancing. He walked a little further and he found skins lying behind a rock, soft, silky seal skins and he knew that these were from seal people, seals from the sea who had taken human form just for one night so that they could dance upon the sand. He was so lonely that he stayed behind the rock all night to watch them dance.

One seal person was more beautiful than all the rest, and the fisherman watched her all night, and as he watched, he fell in love.

As dawn broke and the sun came up, the seal people stopped dancing, ran down the sand, pulled on their seal skins and dived back into the sea where they belonged. All except one. The most beautiful seal woman of them all could not find her seal skin. And she could not find it because the fisherman had hidden it in his pocket.

The seal woman ran to the fisherman and told him she had lost her seal skin and begged him to help her find it so that she could go back to the sea, where she belonged.

The fisherman looked at the seal woman and told her that he had lost his heart to her and begged her to stay with him and to be his wife.

The seal woman looked at the fisherman with pity and love in her deep dark eyes and she said yes, she would stay with him, but she could only stay for seven years. At the end of that time, she said, she would have to return to the sea, where she belonged, or she would surely die.

The fisherman agreed and the two of them were married the very next day.

Every day after that, the fisherman and his seal wife walked together along the beach. They looked out over the sea, and they enjoyed the peace of the evening, and they listened to the sound of the waves on the shore, and their hearts were filled with happiness.

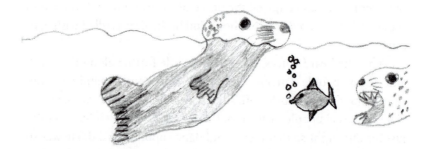

In time, they had children and together the family would walk along the beach. They would look out over the sea and enjoy the peace of the evening and listen to the sound of the waves on the shore, and their hearts would be filled with happiness.

But at the end of the seven years the seal wife began to miss the sea. Her skin became dry, her hands and her feet began to hurt, her deep dark seal eyes became cloudy and she began to find it harder to go for walks along the beach. At last, one day, she went to the fisherman and asked him to give her back her seal skin. The fisherman looked at her and could not bear the thought of losing her, and he said 'no'.

After that, the seal woman stayed home alone more and more, leaving her husband and family to walk along the beach without her. One day, the fisherman and his children went down to the beach, leaving the seal wife in the cottage. While they were gone, to take her mind off the pain in her hands and her feet, she began to clean the house, and while she was cleaning she found a key, hidden in an old jug. It was the key to a wooden chest that the fisherman always kept locked. She took the key and unlocked the chest. She opened the lid and there, inside, was her seal skin.

The fisherman and his children were walking together along the beach. They looked out over the sea and enjoyed the peace of the evening and listened to the sound of the waves on the shore. But that evening their hearts did not fill with happiness but with fear because there, running down the sand, was their mother and she was wearing her seal skin.

The seal woman dived into the water and disappeared beneath the waves, and they thought that they would never see her again. But her head bobbed up out of the water, and she looked at her children with love and pity in her deep dark eyes, and she told them that she loved them and would always remember them.

Then she dived into the water and disappeared beneath the waves, and they thought they would never see her again. But her head bobbed up out of the water once more, and she looked at her husband with love and pity in her deep dark seal eyes, and she told him she loved him, but she had to go back to the sea where she belonged or else she would surely die. She told him that she would always remember him.

Then she dived into the water and disappeared beneath the waves, and they thought they would never see her again.

And nor did they see her again that night. But often, when they were walking along the beach, looking out over the sea, and enjoying the peace of the evening and listening to the sound of the waves on the shore, a head would bob up above the waves and look at them all with love and pity in its deep dark seal eyes and then their hearts would be filled with happiness and they would remember.

Sources

The retellings in the book are all my own but are based on stories from the following sources:

The Story of Today
Storytelling with Children by N. Mellon. Stroud: Hawthorn Press (2000).

Little Red Riding Hood, The Three Little Pigs, Rumpelstiltskin and Hansel and Gretel
all use *The Annotated Classic Fairy Tales* by M. Tatar. London: W.W. Norton & Co. (2002) as a useful first reference.

The Three Feathers
The Complete Illustrated Stories of the Brothers Grimm by J. Grimm and W. Grimm. London: Chancellor Press (1984).

Benno and the Beasts; One of My Geese is Missing
Beasts and Saints by H. Waddell. London: Constable and Co. (1934).

Tom Tit Tot
Tom Tit Tot: An Essay on Savage Philosophy in Folk-Tale by E. Clodd (1898) found at www.sacred-texts.com. *English Fairy Tales* by J. Jacobs. London: Puffin Classics (reissued 1994).

Beira, Queen of Winter
Wonder Tales from Scottish Myth and Legend by D. A. Mackenzie (1917), found at www.sacred-texts.com.

Guru Nanak
This is based on a story I found at www.sikhnet.com.

Never Again
This is based on a newspaper report by J. Romain in *The Times*, 22 January 2005.

The Death of Sigurd the Powerful
Orkneyinga Saga: The History of the Earls of Orkney by H. Pálsson. London: Penguin Classics (1981).

The Wolf and The Seven Little Kids
The Wolf and The Seven Little Kids by V. Southgate. Loughborough: Ladybird Books (1969).

Dear Child
'Cheemuke' by K. Seroney, a storyteller from Kenya, *Facts and Fiction 48*, 18–19 February 2004.

The Selkie Wife
The Mermaid Bride and other Orkney Folk Tales by T. Muir. Kirkwall: Kirkwall Press (1998).

Useful Addresses

Australian Storytelling
A good Australian site is www.australianstorytelling.org, which has further links to international sites, plus interviews, articles and stories.

Lyn Barbour
Lyn is a drama and dance therapist who runs storytelling retreats for teachers. She can be contacted at:
Orkney Images
Via House
Sandwick
Orkney KW16 3JF
Tel: 01856 841207
Website: www.orkneyimages.com

Barbara Carr Consulting Ltd
PO Box 4690
Henley-on-Thames RG9 3ZR
Email: carrbar@btinternet.com

Forest Books
Forest Books specialises in books, videos and CD-ROMs on deafness and deaf issues. The book *Start to Sign!*, by R. Magill and A. Hodgson, can be ordered through them.
Forest Bookshop Warehouse, New Building
Ellwood Road, Milkwall
Colford
Gloucestershire GL16 7LE
Tel: 01594 833858
Email: forest@forestbooks.com
Website: www.forestbooks.com

Godly Play
Information about Godly Play can be found at www.godlyplay.org.
Alison Seaman, an advisor with experience of adapting Godly Play for schools, may be contacted at alison.seaman@alibri.co.uk.

National Storytelling Network
The National Storytelling Network in the US has a website www.storynet.org, which gives advice on storytelling and news about conferences and storytellers.

Society for the Advancement of Philosophical Enquiry and Reflection in Education (SAPERE)
For information or questions:
Lizzy Lewis, Development Officer, SAPERE
Westminster Institute of Education
Oxford Brookes University
Harcourt Hill Campus
Oxford OX2 9AT
Tel: 01865 488340
Fax: 01865 488356
Email: admin@sapere.net
Website: www.sapere.net

Society for Storytelling
The Society for Storytelling is an organisation that aims to promote storytelling and the oral tradition and to provide information about storytelling, stories, storytellers and storytelling events. For more information contact:
Society for Storytelling
PO Box 2344
Reading RG6 7FG
Tel: 0118 935 1381
Website: www.sfs.org.uk

References

Berryman, J.W. (1991) *Godly Play*. Minneapolis: Augsburg.

Bettelheim, B. (1976) *The Uses of Enchantment*. London: Penguin Books.

Bryson, B. (2003) *A Short History of Nearly Everything*. London: Black Swan Books.

Carter, J. (2002) *Cars Stars Electric Guitars*. London: Walker Books.

Fisher, R. (1996) *Stories for Thinking*. Oxford: Nash Pollack Publishing.

Fonagy, P., Steele, M., Steele, H., Higgitt, A. and Target, M. (1994) 'The Emanuel Miller Memorial Lecture 1992: The theory and practice of resilience.' *Journal of Child Psychology and Psychiatry 35*, 2, 231–257.

Fox Eades, J.M. (2004) 'Clarifying Truth with SEN Pupils.' *RE Today*.

Goleman, D. (1996) *Emotional Intelligence*. London: Bloomsbury.

Gray, C. (1994) *The New Social Story Book*. Arlington, TX: Future Horizons.

Gray, G. and Weare, K. (2003) *What Works in Developing Children's Emotional and Social Competence and Wellbeing?* DfES Research Report 456.

Grimm, J. and Grimm, W. (1984) *The Complete Illustrated Stories of the Brothers Grimm*. London: Chancellor Press.

Hartman, B. (2002) *Anyone Can Tell a Story*. Oxford: Lion Publishing.

Haynes, J. (2002) *Children as Philosophers*. London: Routledge/Falmer.

Lewis, C.S. (1955) *The Magician's Nephew*. London: Fontana.

Mackenzie, D.A. (1917) *Wonder Tales from Scottish Myth and Legend*. www.sacred-texts.com.

Magill, R. and Hodgson, A. (2000) *Start to Sign!* London: Royal National Institute for the Deaf.

McKinley, R. (1978) *Beauty and the Beast*. London: Futura Publications.

Pálsson, H. (1981) *Orkneyinga Saga: The History of the Earls of Orkney*. London: Penguin Classics.

Rowe, C. (1999) 'Do social stories benefit children with autism in mainstream primary schools?' *British Journal of Special Education 26*, 1, 12–14.

Scott Littleton, C. (ed.) (2002) *The Illustrated Anthology of World Myth and Storytelling*. London: Duncan Baird Publishers.

Salans, M. (2004) *Storytelling with Children in Crisis: Take Just One Star – How Impoverished Children Heal Through Stories*. London: Jessica Kingsley Publishers.

Seligman, M.E.P. (1990) *Learned Optimism*. London: Free Press.

Seligman, M.E.P. (1995) *The Optimistic Child*. New York: HarperPerennial.

Seligman, M.E.P. (2003) *Authentic Happiness.* London: Nicholas Brealey Publishing.

Seligman, M.E.P. (2004a) *Content, Serene and Satisfied.* Lecture given as part of Master Class 5, Authentic Happiness Coaching Course Four, www.authentichappinesscoaching.com, 2 December 2004.

Seligman, M.E.P. (2004b) *Three Blessings.* Master Class 4, Authentic Happiness Coaching Course Four, www.authentichappinesscoaching.com, 18 November 2004.

Starkey, D. (2001) *Elizabeth.* London: Vintage.

Tatar, M. (2002) *The Annotated Classic Fairy Tales.* London: W.W. Norton & Co.

Trivizas, E. and Oxenbury, H. (1993) *The Three Little Wolves and the Big Bad Pig.* London: Egmont Books.

Waddell, H. (1934) *Beasts and Saints.* London: Constable and Co.

Wright, A. (2000) *Spirituality and Education.* London: Routledge/Falmer.

Subject Index

3–5–7 technique 77
adaptation, of story 21
adolescents *see* older children; teenagers
adults, characterised in stories 37
Advent 91, 99–100
affirmation, in group work 62–3
age
    and traditional stories 40–2
    see also older children; teenagers
anecdotal storytelling
    by adults 12
    by children 57
anger 120, 121
'anima' stories 87–8
    creation myths 89
Annotated Classic Fairy Tales, The 42, 74
anxieties, role of stories 37–8, 51, 73–4
art teaching, using stories 113–14
ASD (autistic spectrum disorder), use of
    social stories 53–4
Asperger's syndrome, use of social stories
    53
audience
    adaptation to 15, 16, 19
    participation of 27
autistic spectrum disorder (ASD), use of
    social stories 53–4
awareness of others 133, 134

bad events, in stories 50–1
Beira, Queen of Winter 89, 90, 92–4
Benno and the Beasts 54–6
British Sign Language 27

cards technique, for emotional vocabulary
    building 122–5
characters
    children from audience as 52,
        99–100

identification with 34
    portrayal of adults 37
children
    as characters in stories 52, 99–100
    as storytellers 57–69
children's stories, therapeutic power 9
choice
    in creating stories 77
    of stories 43
        for beginner storytellers 20
        children's involvement in 58, 78
        empowerment 54
climate, stories explaining 85
collections, using in stories 87
collective stories 48–9
communication, through storytelling 15
community, of storytellers in school 28
comparison
    creation myths 89–90
    versions of stories 76–7
constellations, use of stars in stories 89
creation myths 89–90
creativity in storytelling 14
    encouraging in children 15, 16–17,
        52
cross-cultural versions, of stories 74–6,
    114
cultural heritage 34
curriculum
    use of storytelling 11–12, 105–14
    see also national curriculum

daily repetition of stories 26
darkness, fear 88–9
Dear Child 116–18
death, in traditional stories 38–9
Death of Sigurd the Powerful, The 107
depression 34–5, 132, 137
descriptive sentences, in social stories 53
digital photography, use with story boxes
    112
directive sentences, in social stories 53
drama, in storytelling 25
drawing, to record stories 65–6

Easter 91
emotional development, and philosophy
    72–3
emotional literacy 16, 119–28
emotional vocabulary 122–5
emotions
    conflicting 126–7
    exploring through stories 73–4,
        120–1, 124
    included in event stories 50–1
    and learning 14, 119–20
    mixed 126–7, 134–5
    projection onto stories 38
    role of traditional stories 37, 39, 43
empowerment
    by making choices 78
    satisfaction of storytelling 54, 63
endings
    happy, in fairy tales 35
    at school, reflective stories 139, 140
environment
    using collections from 87
    stories about 85–6, 87–92
    for storytelling 22, 86
events, creating stories from 49–51
evil, in traditional tales 33, 38

fairy tales 12, 33, 35
    see also traditional stories
farewells 140
fear
    of darkness 88–9
    in response to stories 39–40
feasts, in Godly Play 97
feedback, to children using reflective
    stories 136–7
festivals, use in storytelling 90–2
flexibility, in storytelling 16
food, role in religious communities 97
freeze frame technique, emotions in stories
    124

geology, birth of science 109
gestures, for children to perform 27–8
Godly Play 23, 96–7
Goldilocks 127–8
'good bits/bad bits' technique 132–4,
    134–5
good and evil, in traditional tales 33, 38
group feelings 127–8
group stories 48–9
group work, on traditional stories 59–62
Guru Nanak 98–9

handwriting, in scribing stories 48–9
Hansel and Gretel 124–5, 128–30
happy endings, in fairy tales 35
harvest festivals 91
hate 38, 39, 120, 121
history teaching, using stories 106–8, 113
holocaust, and story of hope 101
Hood, Robin, legend 107–8
hope
    stories of 100–1
    in traditional tales 35
Hutton, James 109
hypothetical questions, explored through
    stories 73–4

inclusiveness, in storytelling 15
individuality, of storyteller 25
informal storytelling 19
interaction
    in storytelling 14–15
    see also responsiveness
interpretation of stories, by listener 36–7,
    42–3
introverted children, storytelling by 57–8
involvement of children
    in choice of stories 54, 58, 78
    in storytelling 15

joke telling 19
journey technique, to record stories 65

Kojetin, holocaust 101

learning
    and emotions 14, 119–20
    through stories 53–4
legends 107–8
    see also myths
life stories 13
light and dark 88–9
listening to children 57
listening skills 62–3, 111
literacy, use of stories 112
Little Red Riding Hood 27, 29–31,
    133–4
Lowell, Percival 108
Lowell Observatory 108

map technique, to record stories 65
maths teaching, using stories 109–10, 112
meaning, interpretation of stories 36–7,
    42–3
mental illness, depression 34–5, 132, 137
metaphors
    for powerful emotions 73
    using props as 60
    in traditional tales 35–6
mind maps 41, 59, 76, 132, 134
mixed emotions 126, 134–5
models, for creating new stories 47–8
Montessori method, Godly Play 96–7
mood of class, and responsiveness 48,
    127–8
moral development, using stories 113
morality, in traditional tales 33–4
multi-sensory storytelling 15, 98–9
music teaching, using stories 113
myths 34
    creation 89–90
    see also legends

Name of the Helper story, versions 75, 76,
    77, 78–81

names
    using children's own in stories 52
    in traditional stories 34
national curriculum
    and storytelling skills 17
    see also curriculum
National Storytelling Week 29, 91
Never Again 101
new stories *see* unique stories
news stories 100
Norse sagas 106–7

older children
    play in storytelling sessions 61
    story tennis 64
    and traditional stories 41
One of My Geese is Missing 102–4
optimistic thinking, use of stories 132–4
oral tradition, storytelling 11
Orkneying Saga 106–7
others, awareness of 133, 134
outside environment, for storytelling 86

Performing Arts Week 91
personality, of storyteller 25
perspective sentences, in social stories 53
pessimism 132
philosophy for children 71–4
    for religious education 96
play sessions, in storytelling by children
    61–2
Pluto, discovery of planet 108
point of view
    of audience 133
    characters in stories 125–6, 134–5
positive listening 62–3
praise, specificity of 63
professional storytelling 13
projection, of emotions onto stories 38
props 22–3, 23–4, 60, 65
psychology, use of stories 13, 35

rain sticks, to create atmosphere 22
reading aloud 13
recitation 20
recording stories
    through drawing 65–6
    of teachers' experiences 140
    in writing 50, 139
reflection
    on stories 71, 97
    in teaching 131–2, 139–40
reflective stories 135–40
relationships
    effect of including child's name 52
    effect of storytelling 28, 42
religious education (RE) 95–102
religious stories 12, 95–104
repetition 25–6
    fulfilling a need 36–7
    variation in 26, 29
responsiveness
    to mood 48, 127–8
    in storytelling 14–15
Robin Hood (legend) 107–8
Rumpelstiltskin (Name of the Helper story)
    75, 76, 77, 78–81

sacred stories 12, 95–104
saints' stories 102
SAPERE 72
saying goodbye 140
scarves, symbol for storyteller 62, 64
science teaching, using stories 108–9, 113
scribing, group stories 48–9
seasons, in storytelling 90
self-esteem, and satisfaction of storytelling
    63
Selkie Wife, The 91, 123–4, 126, 134–5,
    141–4
'sense' stories 86
senses, multi-sensory storytelling 98–9
shy children, storytelling by 57–8
sign language 27

silence
    creating 21–2
    following storytelling 71
    on listening walks 86
    in story box technique 24
Snow White 40–1
social skills, developed through group
    storytelling 60–1
social stories 53–4
Society for the Advancement of
    Philosophical Enquiry and Reflection in
    Education (SAPERE) 72
'sound' stories 86
speaking and listening skills 111
special needs children 15, 98–9
    enjoyment of repetition 26
    use of social stories 53–4
spiritual development 95
    using stories 113
'splitting off', of emotions 121
stars (astronomy/astrology) 89
story box technique 23–5, 89
    use of digital photography 112
    with groups 60
Story of Today 17, 137–8
story tennis 64
storytelling days 28, 29
subjects, use of storytelling 105–14

teaching
    importance of reflection 131–2,
        139–40
    using stories in curriculum 11–12,
        106–14
teamwork, encouraging in children 61
techniques
    3–5–7 for thinking skills 77
    for atmosphere creation 22
    for audience participation 27
    drawing stories 65–6
    emotional vocabulary building 122–5
    for optimistic thinking 132–4
    using props 22–3, 23–4, 60, 65

story boxes *see* story box technique
story tennis 64
telling stories outside 86
WWW activity 63, 138–9
teenagers
    using stories with 9, 40–1
    see also older children
therapeutic use, of stories 9, 35, 40–1
thinking skills 71–8
    and reflection 135
Three Billy Goats Gruff 42, 110–11
Three Blessings exercise 138
Three Feathers, The 44–5
Three Little Pigs 20, 36, 38–9, 66–9, 72,
    73–4
Three Pigs Plus (game) 41–2
Tom Tit Tot 81–4
Tombaugh, Clyde 108
traditional stories 12, 33–45
    changing details 20
    and saying goodbye 141
    in subject teaching 106–8, 110–14
    told by children 58–60

unfinished stories 52
unique stories, creation 47–56, 64–6

variation, in repetition of stories 26, 29
versions, of stories 74–6, 76–7, 114
Viking invasion 106
violence, in traditional stories 38–40
vocabulary, for emotions 122–5

Waldorf education system 26
walks, to create stories 86–7
wand technique, to record stories 65–6
weather
    using in storytelling 88
    see also climate
Werburga 102–4
'What Went Well' activity 63, 138–9
Wolf and the Seven Little Kids, The
    111–16

'wondering questions', Godly Play 97
writing down stories 48–9, 50, 139
WWW activity 63, 138–9

Zeigarnik effect 140
zodiac stories 89

Author Index

Berryman, J.W. 96, 97, 99
Bettelheim, B. 35, 40
Bryson, B. 108, 109

Carter, J. 89

Fisher, R. 124
Fonagy, P. 63, 131, 133
Fox Eades, J.M. 98

Goleman, D. 119, 122
Gray, C. 53
Gray, G. 119
Grimm, J. 44
Grimm, W. 44

Hartman, B. 52
Haynes, J. 72
Hodgson, A. 27

Lewis, C.S. 34, 89

Mackenzie, D.A. 89
Magill, R. 27
McKinley, R. 13

Oxenbury, H. 20

Pálsson, H. 107

Rowe, C. 53

Salans, M. 48
Scott Littleton, C. 90
Seligman, M.E.P. 14, 34, 132, 138
Starkey, D. 106

Tatar, M. 42, 74, 75, 114
Trivizas, E. 20

Waddell, H. 52
Weare, K. 119
Wright, A. 96